AN INTRO-GUIDE TO A SEX POSITIVE YOU

Lessons, Tales, and Tips

by Yael Rosenstock

Publisher, Kaleidoscope Vibrations, LLC

Dedication

This is dedicated to all of the people who have felt shame, confusion, and fear in relation to sex and sexuality. It's for those who have been called names like slut, prude, or sissy. It's for anyone who has been coerced, forced, or in any way made to engage in unwanted sexual activity.

This book is dedicated to all the people who are taking control and ownership of their sexuality. It's for those who are proud to be the sexual beings they are, however they come. It's for those who want to create only positive sexual experiences for those with whom they have sex.

This book is dedicated to all the versions of me I have been and will be: ashamed, frightened, intimidated, confused, hurt, fierce, sexy, powerful, queen.

Foreword

I met Yael Rosenstock when my colleague Diana Romero and I were co-teaching an intimate seminar at the CUNY Graduate Center on the topic of sexual and reproductive wellness, health disparities, and social inequity. It was eight of us, all cisgender women but with a wide variety of sexual identities and coming from all different educational, ethnic, religious, language, and class backgrounds and walks of life outside of this classroom that we occupied together. We shared a commitment to inclusive feminism and to a pro-pleasure, gender-diverse, and sexually non-prescriptive goal of working toward ensuring the best health possible for as many people as possible. It's actually a practical, even modest, goal, but one that can feel like a receding and fantastical horizon as more and more political and economic obstacles pile up to keep us from reaching it.

Hand-in-hand along with these shared commitments and goals was the fact that we were all teachers working together. Two of us were there as professors and six as students, but we were all learning together and learning better how and why to teach. The course was supported by the Futures Initiative at the Graduate Center, which works to develop community college educators, to help public college and university instructors reach more students and find more fulfillment in their jobs, and these connected objectives – to teach, to learn, to collaborate, and to strive towards fulfillment in all senses – shaped this amazing seminar experience for all of us. It became one of those rare, precious educational experiences that can be galvanizing and transformative. We all made that phenomenon happen together, but Yael was a major driving force and catalyst that made the seminar particularly meaningful.

Yael has a wonderful ability to really listen and hear what those around her are saying and to get her ideas across to them. She seems to thrive on working with others and making conversations happen. In our seminar, she slid in and across the roles of supporter, helper, student, teacher, colleague, critic when necessary, and friend, and I know that in her work with young folks, she becomes a mentor and guide as well. It's this eagerness and natural ability to communicate along with her commitment to openness and education that make her exactly the right person to write this guide. And this guide is very necessary right now.

We live in this cultural moment of great possibility in the lives of so many people, of this growing cross-section of society that is sophisticated and curious about sexuality and gender, of more open-mindedness to the many kinds of lives and relationships and families people can have, and of better comprehension of what social justice and equity might look like in our intimate lives and why that matters. All this exciting opportunity and growth, though, can also feel confusing and destabilizing, and it's all faced by a political backlash that seems to seek to silence and stifle and divide. It can be a murky terrain for young people (or older folks) to negotiate, and having a practical, knowledgeable, caring guide through it all is an invaluable resource. Yael is an excellent person to step up to provide some insight and clarity. This book offers information, suggestions, and guidelines to help readers find and advocate for their own pleasure and happiness and to treat partners and others graciously, honestly, and ethically. It's a recipe for sexual well-being and personal health.

I'm a teacher by profession, a passionate believer in the pursuit and practice of public health as essential to a good society full of secure, well, and informed people. Knowledge really is power, and Yael is offering her readers a genuinely useful path to personal empowerment and better personal health with this guide. I think you'll appreciate her warm, thoughtful, and knowledgeable voice as much as I do.

Dr. Ananya Mukherjea

Preface

I consider myself someone who has been sexual from close to day one. While I don't have early memories of masturbation, I have a long history of fantasizing about partnered romantic and sexual activities. My parents tell the story of my coming home from the neighbor's house at 2 years old gleefully sharing that I had my first kiss (read: peck on the lips) with an older (5-year-old) boy. That experience fueled years of fantasies as documented by the sporadic journaling of my child-self imagining swimming in a pool and making out with him years after he had moved away.

My second kiss (read: second lip peck) occurred during kindergarten in the first row of the church pews where my classmates and I began our mornings 5 days a week. As everyone was starting to stand for the next prayer, we ducked, kissed, and then joined the rest. While my first kiss with tongue wouldn't happen until many years later, I had plenty of crushes and romantic notions in my head of what could occur with the boys I knew (fantasies involving women didn't occur until later). Reflecting as an adult, this history of fantasizing, coupled with the warm sensations in my lower stomach as I watched images on TV that spoke to my now identifiably kinky tendencies, led me to recognize my sexual nature.

[Sexual Assault Trigger Warning]

My first full on kiss happened at 14. Though young, I had already developed a complex about my sexuality. Specifically, I felt like I had somehow fallen behind my peers by not having had my first real kiss. It didn't help that my first kiss was with

James[1], a boy who had had multiple girlfriends and shared with me his reputation as an excellent kisser causing me anxiety about my own performance and prowess. Unfortunately, I made up for my inexperience by rushing into sexual acts. My boyfriend, excited by the idea of us engaging in any type of sexual experience, began to pester me constantly about when he would be receiving his first blow job. I was neither eager nor ready. I had been giving him hand jobs between abandoned shelves at a nearby library and when we were alone at his place but had never fully considered the act of placing my mouth around his penis. For a while, I just brushed it off, dismissed his questions and requests with as much ease as I could muster. But then one day, James asked the question again while we sat in the back row of a dark movie theater. I was tired of constantly rejecting his requests and remained silent. This time, I couldn't find the voice to say no outright. I felt exhausted by the need to repetitively state my boundaries and the fact that they weren't being respected. My silence was interpreted as consent, or at least good enough, and the next thing I knew, my head was being pushed down onto his dick.

To this day I struggle with calling this assault. I could have fought, I could have continued saying no, I could have bit his penis as hard as possible. I loved him though, with that intense and blinding love that accompanies first relationships, and I just obliged. That became a traumatic memory and a traumatic relationship that took me years to work through afterwards with future men. In fact, through the process of writing this book and the #metoo movement, I discovered it is still something that affects me. **[Trigger Warning Over]**

---

[1] Names of characters and contributors have been changed unless otherwise requested.

James was my first hard lesson in coercive sex. Unfortunately, he was far from my only negative sexual experience. My negative and positive experiences have helped shape who I am. I have always been a resource for sex-related questions to those around me and I realized that through writing this guide, I could increase my impact. I envision a world free of sexual violence and full of sexually empowered individuals. This guide, though painful to write, is one of my contributions towards that vision.

This book is for people of any gender to learn how to engage in exciting, consensual, and pleasurable sex. I particularly hope that those of us who have been socialized to ignore our needs find some freedom through this book. For those who have been socialized that it is okay to ignore the needs of others, I hope this book helps you recognize the importance of respecting and caring for fellow humans, regardless of who they are to you.

Though my personal narratives, and those of others, remain gendered, the statements, tips, and recommendations use gender inclusive language to honor the many ways in which we love, are loved, hurt, and are hurt. Anyone of any gender can be aggressive, assertive, passive, or victimized so we cannot erase the experiences of those who are not assumed to be potential victims. At the same time, we must be aware that most violence, sexual and other, is done by cis-men and that most of the sexual violence is against womxn (cis and transwomen). Therefore, we must be intentional in how we strive for sex positivity and the elimination of sexual violence.

> Womxn is a term that was created to represent the inclusion of transwomen and women of color who have been, and continue to be, left out of [white] feminist movements.

Acknowledgements

There are many people who have helped me get to this point. I am incredibly fortunate to have a supportive family, work environment, and friends who believe in me. I have also benefited from access to programs, jobs, and volunteer positions that have broadened my knowledge on sex positivity and trauma. But before my experiences, professional and personal, there was my mother, Miledy.

Partnered sex was a topic constantly discussed in our home and on car rides. Mom was determined that her three daughters would feel prepared when faced with sexual situations. For my mother, sex is something beautiful between people that care deeply for one another in a romantic way. Though she did not encourage early sexual activity, I appreciate that she never pretended sex only happened between married couples. She was realistic in knowing she wouldn't be able to predict or decide for us when our first sexual experiences would occur and instead answered all our questions and insisted sex was an appropriate topic to be discussed. I did experience sexual trauma, but it would have been much worse if I had grown up in a home that hid information from me or shamed my sexuality. My mother built a space in which I felt comfortable asking questions and sharing my experiences. I now help create those spaces for others.

I want to thank my sister, Arielle, who despite our differences, never hesitates to support me. Even when she doesn't agree with me, she has been known to champion my opinions in defense of both me and strangers when we are not around to stand for ourselves. I am proud of the woman she has become. Also, shout out to her being the make-up artist and photographer for my author's image!

Thank you to my current and former partners who have helped shape my experiences and brought me to this point. Whether good or bad, those experiences have led me here. A special thanks to my primary partner, Gael, who supports, loves, and accepts me as I am.

Thank you to Dr. Ananya Mukherjea for not only writing the foreword but for her consistent support of my work. Her words have helped me have the confidence to share this with all of you.

This book would not have been possible without the amazing editing team that rallied in support of me. Carmine Couloute, Marcia Suarez, and David Dudovitz have been instrumental in broadening my understanding of perspectives and identities that I don't hold. Carmine always provides a calming aura which has gotten me through a number of challenging days. Marcia has been my partner and friend through various projects and is always gently letting me know when my work is not as inclusive as I intended for it to be. David, in a short time, has taught me an astounding amount and has inspired me to begin creating workshops that address voices not fully represented in this Intro-guide. Annafi Wahed, founder of a bipartisan news source, the Flipside, drew my attention to missing narratives while also helping me cut pieces that were repetitive. Paola Peña gave me the ego boost I needed towards the beginning of my editing process when she requested I translate the book into Spanish so her mother could read it. Oliver Estrella graciously agreed to edit the book though we had only recently met. In doing so, he provided valuable input, particularly as someone less familiar with me and my work. Christine (Chrissy) Ramkarran was part of my initial inspiration to write a book after she published *Relic*, a powerful collection of poems under the name Christine Amrita. She edited two drafts during the Intro-guide's journey always helping me improve the order and flow. Katherine Kolios, who served as my last content editor, has been editing my work for much of our friendship, which now spans over 15 years. She is an amazing writer and editor and I hope to co-author a piece with her soon. The Intro-guide has grown and improved through the recommendations of this amazing team and would not be where it is now without them.

Lastly, thank you to those who contributed as voices, or storytellers, to the book. Because of you, the Intro-guide benefits from a level of diversity in the narratives that offer readers an opportunity to personally relate to the material. I am grateful that you chose to share pieces of your interior selves with us.

Introduction

When I decided to write this book, a romantic partner questioned the need saying, "books on having great sex are a dime a dozen." His comment forced me to think hard about what my addition to the small, though vital, world of sex positive guides would be. I believe that each of our journeys inspires and influences the ways in which we navigate sexual spaces and realized that the more stories told the better. We may not relate to every moment of a person's lived experiences, but each time an individual chapter or moment is shared, it invites listeners and readers to see pieces of themselves reflected. Though our paths are unique, we can build connection and community among the fragments of isolated experiences. Throughout the development of this book and my work as a sex educator, I have connected with countless individuals who have seen themselves reflected in my stories or who I've felt connected to because of theirs. This is why my own narratives, as well as those of others, can be found across the book. The lessons I share throughout this guide were mostly learned the hard way, and I am eager to share them so that others can avoid (or find community from) similar feelings of relationship and/or sexual trauma and discomfort.

I want to begin this book by saying that not all sexual encounters are going to be steamy and memorable and that's OK, too. Just remember, bad sex when defined as unpleasurable or unexciting is still an opportunity for learning. Bad sex when painful, frightening, or upsetting is what we seek to avoid through the tips in this book. I am grateful to say that by following the techniques laid out in this guide, I have been able to avoid painful, frightening, and upsetting sex. I've also been able to stay away from "unfun" sex because I taught myself to concentrate on my mental, emotional, and physical needs. We cannot control the actions of others that may lead to traumatic or upsetting sex and we are not to blame when it occurs but by prioritizing my emotional needs, I have been able to reduce my fear when experiencing a flashback or feeling triggered.

Positive and pleasurable sex requires the active and willing involvement of mind and body, as well as heart for some. Often, once the mind is aroused, the physical will follow. For others, the physical responses may occur before the mind or heart is ready. For others still, they occur almost simultaneously. Part of engaging in fulfilling and responsible sex is identifying and honoring your own needs and those of the people with whom you're having sex. Part I of the Intro-guide works on developing self-awareness. Part II concentrates on communication and consent: how to develop the tools necessary to voice your desires and boundaries while respecting those of others. Lastly, Part III provides a brief overview of 'need to know' material as well as recommendations for exploration and discovery.

It has been a long journey that is still in progress to acknowledge and embrace all the aspects of my sexuality. It is a struggle to share so much of myself knowing that I want this book to be read by so many. I am not used to this level of vulnerability but I believe it is important to share so that you may see yourself reflected in parts of my story and become open in your own life. I have only come this far by being able to speak candidly to trusted friends and lovers who embraced and supported me in my self-discovery. If even one of you, as readers, can seek support in your self-development as a result of this Intro-guide, this book will have been worth it.

Message from Author

This Intro-guide serves as an introduction to a variety of possibilities and opportunities for self-discovery and exploration as well as reflections on my own experiences and those of others. It is possible that you'll feel uncomfortable reading certain sections or triggered by others. If your discomfort is caused by something new or strange for you, I urge you to keep reading. This book creates a safe way to consider ideas you may have previously avoided or considered taboo. You do not need to try anything you do not wish to try, but exposure to ideas will help you consider new possibilities that may serve you.

For those who have experienced trauma, it is important that you take care of yourself while reading anything that may remind you of your own experiences. Writing this book triggered memories of my own trauma and required that I take breaks for self-care. I added **[TW]** before stories or examples where sexual assault is discussed so you may choose to read or continue through. **[TW-O]** signifies that the example is done. Please engage in your own self-care techniques both in reading this book and in your life overall.

There are also many references to body parts, specifically genitalia, throughout the book to avoid associating body parts with genders. We all have different names for what exists between our legs so what one person might call a clit or cunt, another might call a penis. I use terms like "people with penises" for those who are born with a penis and related genitalia or have had them constructed. This term recognizes that not all men are born with penises and not all people who have penises are men. Therefore, particularly when referencing stimulating genitalia, this will be used in lieu of a gendered term.

Similarly, I use "people with vulvas/vaginas/clits" for persons who are born with vaginas and clitorises or have had them constructed. This term recognizes that not all women are born with vaginas and not all people who have vaginas are women. Though I respect all names associated with a body part, I am generalizing for the sake of consistency within this text. I know that for some the reference to genitalia may be triggering, for which I apologize. I welcome feedback on how to address this for future iterations of the Intro-guide and am grateful to my editors who have helped me think through how to best approach this.

Table of Contents

PART I:

SELF-AWARENESS

I was the girl on the train that gave up her seat to men. I battled boys one and half times my size in painful duels on the playground. I carried my own bags even when it hurt my already damaged back and strong young men offered to take the load. I saw myself as strong, independent, and fierce. Then I met Julian, a German gentleman who, somewhat against my nature, taught me that I am a queen. He upheld traditional hetero ideals of paying for dinner and carrying my heavy items but more than that, Julian showed me what it's like to be sexually ravished for hours. I learned to lose count of my own ejaculations and to put towels down to protect the bed without a sense of shame. There was admittedly awkwardness around the non-sexual aspects of the doting, feminizing, and worship I received. However, I got over my resistance and learned it's good to be Queen!

I pride myself in being a strong, independent, and fierce woman but I learned there are ways in which I appreciate being cared for, assisted, or treated. My power comes from acknowledging and respecting those preferences. Over the years I have learned a lot about myself, my needs, and my wants. This has included my sexuality, my partnering style, my sexual identities, and relationship boundaries. As with other identities, these have the potential to change and grow but for now, it feels secure and grounded to be in touch with myself as I am today. This section of the book focuses on discovering and identifying the self in relation to sex.

CHAPTER 1

Pillow People, Worshippers, & Everyone in Between

One of the preferences I learned courtesy of Julian's teachings, was that I'm meant to be with partners who not only love my body, but also love eliciting pleasure from it. When choosing partners who have penises, I identify as a *cushion lover* (see pages 6-7) because I love being eaten out regularly but don't feel a desire to perform blowjobs with nearly as much regularity. The pleasure of my partner is incredibly important to me, however, and so I intentionally choose partners whose pleasure is linked to me enjoying myself knowing that they will receive physical pleasure during penetrative acts. With partners that have vulvas my identity changes to an *even-steven* because I want to be able to elicit the same pleasure in them as they do for me which generally only occurs through reciprocation.

Usually, before I have sex with people, I have conversations to gauge their sexual needs and exchange style. For those of us who are sexual, there is a spectrum of sexual identities specific to sexual exchange that can range from Pussy/Dick/Genitalia/Body Worshippers to Pillow People (princesses, princes, and persons). I want to note that there can be a lot of stigma associated with these terms depending where you fall, especially with pillow people. The key is to find people who are compatible with this part of your sexual identity and to check in with them regularly to make sure they feel cared for, wanted, and appreciated.

Where do you fall on the Pillow Person to Worshipper Scale?

Answer each question as honestly as you can. Be real. It is likely that you already have a good sense of where you fall on this scale but perhaps you have difficulty articulating it (or maybe you don't!). Regardless of the value you place on your responses, it's useful information about yourself. You may also find that you have different identities in different circumstances. Use the questions as a guide to determine where you land on the spectrum and which of the descriptions feels most fitting for you. If you are not currently sexually active, use past experiences or assumptions about how you may feel in the future.

1. *When you are getting ready to masturbate, you watch/read/imagine you (or a character who would represent you) going down on someone*

   (1) Always   *(2) Often*   *(3) Sometimes*

   (4) Rarely   *(5) Never*   *(6) Only with a specific someone*

2. *When you are getting ready to masturbate, you watch/read/imagine someone going down on you (or someone who would represent you in the scene)*

   (1) Always   *(2) Often*   *(3) Sometimes*

   (4) Rarely   *(5) Never*   *(6) Only with a specific someone*

3. *Your ultimate sexual scene involves acrobatic/aerobic moves from all parties involved.*

4

(1) Always   *(2) Often*   *(3) Sometimes*

(4) Rarely   *(5) Never*   *(6) Only with a specific someone*

4. *Your ultimate sexual scene involves minimal effort or self-propelled movement from yourself.*

     (1) Always   *(2) Often*   *(3) Sometimes*

     (4) Rarely   *(5) Never*   *(6) Only with a specific someone*

5. *You enjoy planning sexual experiences and all the ways you can please your partner and fulfill their desires, whether or not it involves direct contact with your genitalia.*

     (1) Always   *(2) Often*   *(3) Sometimes*

     (4) Rarely   *(5) Never*   *(6) Only with a specific someone*

6. *During sex, you expect to lay back, have your partner please you, and for them to be pleased by your pleasure.*

     (1) Always   *(2) Often*   *(3) Sometimes*

     (4) Rarely   *(5) Never*   *(6) Only with a specific someone*

7. *Giving your partner a handjob or oral sex excites and arouses you.*

     (1) Always   *(2) Often*   *(3) Sometimes*

     (4) Rarely   *(5) Never*   *(6) Only with a specific someone*

8. *Giving your partner a handjob or oral sex feels like a chore or responsibility.*

(1) Always   (2) Often   (3) Sometimes

*(4) Rarely   (5) Never   (6) Only with a
                                      specific someone*

9. *Your partner's(') pleasure is important to you.*

(1) Always   (2) Often   (3) Sometimes

*(4) Rarely   (5) Never   (6) Only with a
                                      specific someone*

10. *Your pleasure is your main concern.*

(1) Always   (2) Often   (3) Sometimes

*(4) Rarely   (5) Never   (6) Only with a
                                      specific someone*

Results

Total Pillow Person - (You chose "always" or "often" for all or most of Questions 2, 4, 6, 8, & 10 while answering "never" or "rarely" for all or most of Questions 1, 3, 5, 7. You choose "sometimes," "rarely," or "never" for Question 9)

You like to lay back and have your body ravished. You see sex with you as the source of pleasure for others or possibly don't care about the pleasure of others. Either way, a good sexual experience involves your orgasm occurring through direct attention. The other person may orgasm through minimal effort on your part or perhaps not at all.

Cushion Lover - (You chose "often" for all or most of Questions 2, 4, 6, & 10 and "sometimes" or "often" for Question 8 while answering "rarely" or "sometimes" for all or most of Questions 1, 3, 5, & 7). You chose "often" or "always" for Question 9.
You, like a pillow person love to receive. However, your partner's pleasure is important to you and you enjoy knowing that they

are enjoying themselves. You may prefer that their enjoyment involve less action on your part but you can be enthusiastic about pleasing a partner directly if that is what is needed for their pleasure to be attained.

Even-Steven/Giver-Taker (Your answers can be a complete mixture but generally your responses indicate that you enjoy giving and receiving)

You really enjoy receiving sexual pleasure but you also love pleasuring. You don't really keep score because you are happy to provide if your partner(s) feels the same way. You may begin comparing orgasm counts, however, if you are feeling neglected. On the flipside, you can be excited by the opportunity to "spoil" partner's(') who feel deserving.

Pleasure Doter (You chose "often" for all or most of Questions 1, 3, 5, & 7 and answer "always" or "often" for Question 9, while answering "rarely" or "sometimes" for all or most of Questions 2, 4, 6, & 8, with any response to Question 10)

While you may enjoy receiving pleasure, even being ravished, you really enjoy being the cause of someone else's pleasure. It excites and motivates you to know you can illicit ecstasy in someone else. You enjoy thinking up new and creative ways to please your partner(s).

Pussy/Dick/Body Worshipper (You chose "always" or "often" for all or most of Questions 1, 3, 5, & 7 and answer "always" for Question 9 while answering "never," "rarely," or "sometimes" for all or most of Questions 2, 4, 6, & 8 with any response to question 10)

Like the pleasure doter, your partner(s)'s pleasure is of the utmost importance to you. However, it's more than that. You ADORE and revel in making your partner's(') body(ies) hum with sexual energy. You love to look, taste, touch, and smell. You can spend hours, possibly all day pleasing them and eliciting moans. Your fantasies and masturbation often involve thinking of new ways to excite them. For some, your own pleasure is so directly tied to the pleasure you elicit in others, your own orgasm can be an afterthought.

Person specific: Sometimes there are people in our lives for whom our label switches. We may start off as cushion lovers or Even-Stevens and then with a new partner, become doters and worshippers or pillow persons. Sometimes, it's us discovering who we were all along. Other times, it could be related to that person's scent, or pheromones, the sounds they make, their taste, or how we feel about them emotionally.

I want to add Demi-princess, Demi-cushion-lover, Demi-doter, and Demi-worshipper. I created these terms borrowing from demi-sexual. These would describe individuals who require strong romantic connection before becoming taking or giving partners. Within relationships in which they feel less connected, they may be anywhere else on the spectrum.

The term pillow-princess was developed as a slur for lesbians who do not reciprocate sexually, a "stone femme." However, it has been adapted since then. People of any gender can be a pillow-person. Additionally, though originally intended as a negative nickname, I have spoken with individuals and read blogs about people who enjoy pillow people. However, what sometimes occurs is that if someone has experienced trauma, they may not feel safe engaging in certain acts. It is important to speak with your partners and learn about their experiences and needs. I want to stress that caring for another should be prioritized and determining what that care looks like is the work of those in the relationship.

CHAPTER 2:

Understanding Your Sexualities

We've already discussed the kind of involvement you enjoy within sexual experiences (giver/taker). This section talks about what gets you going. For example, there are demi-sexuals who require an emotional connection to feel arousal. There are those whose arousal is based in powerplay, and others whose sexual focus is on particular body parts – like feet. There are those whose attraction is related to specific genders or sexes and others for whom gender and sex are irrelevant. We all have things that get us going and others that turn us off. Though sexuality commonly refers to sexual orientation, I choose to incorporate everything listed in this paragraph, including being a giver/taker, as part of one's sexuality.

Parts of our sexuality, like the genders we find attractive, are often determined before birth. By that I mean we are generally born with our sexual orientation and eventually, when we start liking people romantically or sexually, we discover our sexual orientation. Other parts of our sexuality can be influenced by our experiences, both positive and negative. As you read about different identities and experiences, embrace the idea of sexual diversity and resist yucking yums. Whether you like or understand something doesn't excuse shaming or dismissing others with different ways of being. You may even discover that you are part of communities you never considered. I chose to highlight some of the non-mainstream sexual identities because those that are normalized are already widely known. I encourage you to explore identities left unexplored or un-identified in this book as you go through your journey.

The Gender(s) of Your Lovers

Sexual orientation describes who you are attracted to. It is generally determined prenatally[2] and becomes apparent to us as we begin to feel attraction. There are individuals who know at a very young age whereas others may grow up and start families before fully recognizing their sexuality. Sexual orientation can sometimes be a journey with multiple stops before finding the identity that most fits. Learning about different sexualities doesn't change yours but what could happen is that you may realize your sexuality is not what you thought it was. You may have been a vanilla sex person until you discovered your kinky tendencies. Such a revelation is different from being "turned" something.

> If a cisman hits on a lesbian, she is still a lesbian. If you are hit on by someone outside of the gender or sex you are attracted to, your sexuality will remain the same. This is a concern of some cis-hetero individuals and has led to anger and violence. Sexuality is not a cold you can catch. Defense of your sexuality should never be used as an excuse for violence against another.

Despite heteronormative expectation that queer individuals must "discover" their sexuality whereas straight people simply exist, it is in fact a discovery for all. However, given that the social norm is straight, it can be more difficult to recognize your identity if you're queer because you don't see yourself represented. It also means that many people assume straightness, which often leads to those who don't identify as straight having to announce their sexuality, or "come out of the closet," to be seen. There is a further marginalization of those who identify outside of the gay/lesbian and straight binary. While using a dating app for womxn seeking womxn, I connected with a biphobic lesbian. She was attracted to me

---

[2] I say generally to not discount the narratives of those whose sexual orientation has been a journey that they feel has been influenced by their lives.

but kept ignoring how I self-identified and using her own labels for me. She also kept bringing my identity up making me feel like my sexual orientation was the central discussion point. Even within the queer community, there exists biphobia and a dislike or mistrust of those who are attracted to more than one gender or sex. Those outside the binary are sometimes called greedy or confused, invalidating our experiences of attraction and love.

If you're curious where you may fit or would like to better understand some of the diversity in sexual identities, check out the following list. I've listed sexual orientations and romantic orientations together for the sake of space, except for asexual and aromantic, as they often suffer more invisibility. Sexual orientation refers to the people to whom you are sexually attracted. Romantic orientation refers to those with whom you'd like to be in a romantic relationship which may or may not differ from sexual orientation. For example, some bisexual individuals are heteroromantic in that they are sexually attracted to different genders but only consider a different gender than their own for long-term romantic pairing.

The below list is not comprehensive. I encourage you to continue seeking out information, especially if you do not feel represented.

Androsexual: Individuals who are attracted to masculine-presenting individuals.

Aromantic: Individuals who do not feel romantic attraction.

Asexual: Individuals who do not experience sexual attraction.

Bicurious: Individuals who are experimenting and are unsure about their attraction to different genders.

Biromantic/Bisexual: Individuals who are attracted to more than one gender. The definition is dependent on the individual and can range from attraction to cismen and ciswomen to attraction to men and women, both cis and trans, and other genders as well. Attraction to different genders does not need to be equally divided to be considered bisexual.

Demiromantic/Demisexual: Individuals who require a strong emotional bond before experiencing a romantic or sexual response.

Gay: Often used to identify men who are attracted only to other men but can refer to anyone attracted exclusively to members of their own sex or gender.

Gynosexual: Individuals who are attracted to feminine-presenting individuals.

Heteroflexible: Individuals who are mostly attracted to those considered their opposite[3] gender but who make exceptions for specific individuals.

Heteroromantic/Heterosexual: Individuals who are attracted to what is traditionally considered the opposite gender.

Homoflexible: Individuals who are generally attracted to people who share their gender but make exceptions for specific individuals.

Homoromantic/Homosexual: Individuals who are attracted to those with whom they share a gender.

Lesbian: Womxn who are attracted only to other womxn.

Queer: Individuals who identify somewhere along the sexual (or gender) spectrum outside of heterosexual (or cisgender). For sexuality, this can include lesbian, gay, bisexual, pansexual, etc. This is a common term used among the younger generation,

---

[3] "Opposite" is used due to the long history of gender being understood as a binary.

however, it was previously used as a slur so older generations are less likely to use it.

Panromantic/Pansexual: Individuals who are attracted to people regardless of gender.

***

An important piece of positive sexuality is having a good outlook of yourself and feeling confident in who you are. For years I struggled with my sexual identification. In high school I identified as 80-85% straight because I knew my interest in Halle Berry and other actresses was more than admiration, it was attraction. I had the same conversation over and over again with a friend over a series of years because I couldn't reconcile being queer while having an aversion to vulvas and vaginas. Even after having a semi-erotic response to a platonic sensual massage with a friend of mine in college, I was convinced that I must still be straight because bisexual wasn't quite right and I wasn't aware of the variety of sexual orientations that existed. It didn't dawn on me until recent years that I had a similar aversion to all genitalia but my coercive sexual experience as a teen had normalized penises.

I eventually discovered that I am in fact queer and switch between identifying as that and pansexual. What that means is that I am attracted to people and personalities regardless of their gender. It is easiest for me to attract and date cismen, possibly because of my extensive history with them, but who I date doesn't change my sexuality.

My experience is not unique. Those who identify as pan, asexual, aromantic, demi-sexual, and other lesser known identities may not immediately recognize how to understand and conceptualize their feelings and experiences because of the lack of representation and discussion. This can cause confusion, discomfort, and a sense of loneliness. If you are struggling to understand yourself, I hope the previous list helped you identify a community in which you may feel understood. Keep in mind that whether or not you find a label that fits you, your experiences are valid. Whether you mostly date one sex over the other, are sexually attracted only when packaged with deep romantic connection, or you never experience sexual attraction at all, follow your instincts.

Vanillas, Kinksters, and BDSM

I vaguely remember sitting in front of the TV as a kid and watching a particular "The Nanny" episode. Mr. Sheffield grabs Fran, the nanny, admonishing her for behaving like a child. He proceeds to throw her over his lap saying that if she insists upon behaving like a child, he'll treat her as such, as he spanks her. Fran protests and yells in her nasal voice and then seems to consider her own arousal at the scenario. I remember this scene, whether dreamt or real because of the sensations it elicited in my body. I was turned on but didn't quite know it due to

> B: Bondage and Discipline
> D: Domination and submission
> S: Sadism
> M: Masochism

inexperience. As I got older, I was specifically drawn to romance novels, and later erotica, that focused on powerplay and submission.

As a young and proud feminist, it was difficult to accept myself as craving submission, even if only in one specific aspect of my life. I consider myself dominant in my overall nature and have been described as commanding, aggressive, and passionate by those who have only recently met me. The juxtaposition caused me confusion and shame. It didn't help that there is debate within the feminist world as to whether submission can be empowering or is inherently degrading. The argument is that submission in any space feeds the patriarchy and therefore adds to womxn's unequal space in the world.

This theory haunted my mind until I had lunch with a friend and his friend. We weren't discussing anyone in particular but the friend questioned whether someone who enjoys sexual submission and powerplay could be a feminist. Her question switched on the part of me that enjoys debate.[4] I argued that telling consenting adults what they can or cannot do, or shaming them for what they do, takes away their power. Knowing yourself and consensually practicing sexual and other personal activities that bring you joy, comfort, or excitement is empowering. Additionally, unlike in general society, individuals involved in kink have explicit conversations about the circumstances and context of submission and domination. Unlike with BDSM, the option of simply opting out of sexist, transphobic, racist, ableist situations does not exist in the general world. There is power involved in choosing when to be submissive and having the option of choosing not to submit. By the end of the conversation she and I both had a new perspective on feminism and submission and the possibility of being both/and rather than either/or.

Vanilla sex or people refer to those who engage in what is considered "traditional" or conventional forms of sex. Just like in kink, there can be intimacy and love or it can be a mainly physical experience. Missionary is probably the most widely recognized sexual position within vanilla sex and it is often imagined between heterosexual couples. However, I challenge vanilla sex as being the norm because I imagine that there is

---

[4] For me, it is easy to explain a situation without judgment when I take myself out of the equation. In my own head I had difficulty identifying as both submissive and feminist but could defend the position of nameless strangers. This is also true of my ability to recognize the validity in sexual assault narratives similar to my own while still struggling to accept myself as a survivor of sexual assault.

a large percentage of people that could be described as vanilla*ish* or kinkster-*light*. These would include people who enjoy incorporating light bondage, blindfolds, foods, temperature play, love taps, unique locations, etc. into their sexual experiences. There is also a very wide range of what is considered kinky but it tends to be a catch all for those who have any type of identifiable fetish and/or are interested in powerplay.

Many people assume that BDSM is only practiced by people who have experienced sexual trauma and that what they do is unhealthy, but BDSM tendencies do not require sexual trauma. My own sexual submission and spankee fetish developed before my negative experiences and therefore would have existed regardless. BDSM can also be a healthy and safe way for individuals who have experienced trauma to interact with it. In particular, engaging in Domination and submission play can create spaces in which survivors convert negative experiences into opportunities to reclaim control over their own sexuality after an assault left them feeling disempowered. For an example narrative, read Rita R.'s story.

*[**TW** – Incest/Sexual assault]*

Rita R.'s Journey to Sexuality

I had always been aware of having been assaulted, but I was in denial of it because my abuser was a family member. So for years, I struggled with my sexuality and my body in general. I did not want to be seen or looked at and turned towards "modesty" as a form of coping (i.e. modest forms of dressing and avoiding sexual encounters that I felt would place me in a submissive position). This gave way to a somewhat obsessive habit where I was constantly preoccupied with controlling my body in multiple ways, such as restrictive eating and grooming, like constantly shaving my body hair. These practices eventually snowballed into an avalanche and I suffered a year of turmoil, filled with panic attacks, breakdowns, and outbursts. Eventually I was able to seek out professional help through the support of my partner. However, while my therapy sessions allowed me to make amends with my emotional demons, my relationship allowed me to make amends with my physical demons. Being that physical intimacy is generally a significant aspect of a romantic relationship, my partner and I explored ways of intimacy that not only produced pleasure for the both of us, but allowed me to feel safe, and by extent, empowered. It was/is during this time of exploration and experience that I realized that submissive play with someone I trust is actually an enjoyable and therapeutic form of sexual play for me. The trust between us alleviates my anxieties that had surrounded the concepts of sex and sexuality, while the submissive play allowed me to deny my compulsion to control my body. [TW-O]

Reflection Questions

1. *If you are not part of the BDSM community, what are your assumptions as an outsider looking in? Has Rita's or my own story of being kinky given you a new perspective? Are there ways you are kinkyish that you have not previously considered?*
2. *If you are a member of the BDSM community, reflect upon the path that brought you to where you are. Do you feel confident in your identities and tastes or do you harbor shame? If the latter, what are ways you can develop a positive sense of self in relation to BDSM?*

If you are interested in identifying your kinks, I recommend going to bdsmtest.org to help categorize you. As with sexual orientation, there are those who may be completely one way or another, but often there are pieces of us that fall into different categories so when we recognize all of our parts, we have the opportunity to explore all of those identities.

There are a great number of ways to be kinky so I'll name some of the common ones on the next few pages. Through exploring a kinky yes/no/maybe/fantasy sheet[5] you can become familiar with many more. Be sure to look up unknown items either alone or with people who will not mind seeing extreme images as some activities involve blood, fecal matter, urine, and other bodily fluids as well as scenes of extreme levels of violence against bodies. I'll start with a breakdown of the acronym of BDSM and add further pieces thereafter.

Bondage refers to any restriction technique. This may include ropes, scarves, ties, etc. The following three rules are important for safe play:

1. Look up techniques for knots that can be easily undone. In the case of an emergency, it is important that the person who is bound can trust the person binding to release them quickly and efficiently. Done well, this will not affect the binding process as there are knots that hold well until pulled a specific way.

2. Do research as to where on the body, and with how much pressure, you can tie someone up. If you do not know what you are doing, it is possible to cause short term as well as permanent nerve damage. This can occur without the bound individual realizing.

---

[5] I will explain more about yes/no/maybe/fantasy sheets in Chapter 5. For an example sheet, see the end of this chapter.

3. Never leave a bound individual alone for long because there is always the danger that they may require something immediate and not be able to escape. This is both because of potential nerve damage that cannot be addressed if the person is immobile and alone as well as other potential physical and mental health concerns.

It is also possible to be mentally bound to someone, as is the case with some of the following dynamics.

Discipline includes the physical and mental methods used to train submissives. This can look like physical punishments, reduced privileges, or humiliation.

Domination/submission refers to power play relationships. There are different levels of engagement ranging from "scenes" in which this dynamic is played out to permanent living conditions. A subset of the Dom(me)/sub dynamic is the Master/slave dynamic which includes almost complete control by one person over another. It is not complete control in that slaves and submissives are willingly consenting and trusting another person to care for them and control them. Therefore, though the Master or Domme is responsible and gives commands, the slave or sub has the option of ending any situation using a predetermined safe word.

Part of giving over trust and control involves engaging in activities that are uncomfortable or almost beyond one's limits. A safe word is used when a situation has gone too far and must end abruptly. Often the use of a safe word leads to immediate "aftercare" being performed. Aftercare includes anything that occurs at the end of the scene or situation to ensure all members involved feel secure and comfortable. I personally like **red** for stop and **yellow** to indicate that a breaking point is being approached. Yellow means the activity in question cannot go any further but also does not need to completely end nor require immediate aftercare.

To the outside world, it can be difficult to understand these dynamics and they may not appear consensual. This is an issue that arises for those who engage in body mutilation and physical punishment when they seek routine medical care. If reported by medical professionals[6], engagement in BDSM can be considered assault or abuse depending on local laws on what is considered behavior one may consent to.

Sadomasochism Sadism refers to those who enjoy inflicting pain upon others while masochism refers to those who get gratification from receiving pain. Both can often manifest sexually. Not surprisingly, these people are able to fulfil one another's needs by incorporating painful experiences into their relationships and sex lives.

Switch is someone who switches between being a Dominant and submissive individual. They may switch within a specific relationship or be a submissive to one person while Dominant to another.

Brats are individuals who fall into the bottom/submissive grouping but are not truly submissive. They intentionally annoy and frustrate their Dominants to manipulate the situation and receive the punishment they seek.

Fetishes come in many forms. They can be natural inclinations as well as inclinations inspired through trauma. Fetishes include sexual fascination with body parts, bodily fluids, specific activities, as well as "types" of people (such as specific body types, races, hair colors, etc.).

---

[6] For a list of BDSM friendly medical and other professionals, see Resources on pages 157 – 158.

Voyeurs are those who enjoy watching others engage in sexual activities.

Exhibitionists enjoy sex in public places and being watched or the risk of being found. Sex parties are ideal for both voyeurs and exhibitionists as they are intended for those activities.

This provided a taste into some of the identities that are contained by the term kinky or BDSM. Others include daddy/baby girl, spankees, doctor/patient, puppies, etc. If you are interested in exploring your kinky sexuality, Fetlife.com serves as a social media platform where you can befriend fellow kinksters, seek out events near you, and watch or read the exploits of others.

Yes/No/Maybe/Fantasy Kink Sheet

This serves an example kink sheet. An actual Y/N/M/F Kink sheet would be numerous pages long. The key explains who is doing the action and who the action is being performed on.

Key
(W) = Wearing (R) Receiving (B) Bottoming
(G) = Giving (T) Topping

Activity	Ever Tried?	Yes - Into	Yes - Willing	Maybe	No	Fantasy
Blindfolds (W)						
Blindfolds (G)						
Flogging[7] (R)						
Flogging (G)						
Orgasm denial[8] (B)						
Orgasm denial (T)						
Pain (R)						
Pain (G)						
Swallowing Cum (R)						
Swallowing Cum (G)						

---

[7] Whipping

[8] Not allowing a partner to orgasm. This can be used as a punishment for unwanted behavior or to demonstrate one's Dominance over a submissive.

CHAPTER 3:

Gender Identities

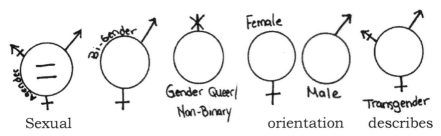

Sexual orientation describes who you are attracted to whereas gender identity is about the gender you identify with. These are often confused, for which I partially blame the acronyms that begin with LGBTQA. While lesbian, gay, bisexual, and asexual all describe sexual and romantic attraction (or lack thereof), Trans, gender-non-conforming, and non-binary all describe gender identities. "Queer" can be used for

If you are unsure about how to address someone, you can ask for their gender pronouns (GP). GP include she, his, them, zhe, etc. Whatever the response, be sure to respect how the person identifies. If unsure, you can avoid pronouns by using the person's name.

It is NOT ok to ask someone what they have between their legs. Remember, gender is about how you identify, not the physical.

sexual orientation as well as gender identity. There is a lot to discuss on this topic including how gender identity is formed, children coming out younger and younger as trans, the work in different countries to counter socialized gender formation, and more. For the Intro-guide we'll stick to highlighting some identities you can use to better understand yourself and those around you.

Like with sexual orientation, gender identity is often determined before birth and we each have journeys in recognizing that identity. For some, the journey is quick and sure. Awareness of gender identity often begins forming around 3 years old. For trans-children who live free of concern of judgment, this is when they begin to come out as having a gender different from their sex at birth. For cis-children, this is also when they begin to identify with the sex-based gender assigned to them at birth. For many individuals, the journey is longer and more challenging and can continue well into adulthood. There are also individuals for whom gender identity is not static and may change from day to day. This can be a part of transitioning or a permanent state.

Below are some basic gender identity related terms to explore if you are unsure about how to identify or if you would like to better understand loved ones and acquaintances. If you do not feel represented by the list below, you should consider doing some more research to find a term that feels right for you.

Agender - An individual who does not identify with a gender.

Bigender - An individual who identifies with two genders either simultaneously or fluctuates.

Cisgender - An individual who identifies with their sex assigned at birth.

Genderfluid - An individual who moves between genders.

Gender Non-Binary/Gender-Queer - An individual who does not identify as a man or a woman.

Transgender - An individual whose gender does not match their sex assigned at birth.

Transsexual - An individual whose gender does not match their sex assigned at birth who elects to undergo gender affirming surgeries.

Transwoman - An individual who was assigned male at birth and identifies as a woman (male to female (MtF)).

Transman - An individual who was assigned female at birth and identifies as a man (female to male (FtM)).

> An easy way to remember how someone identifies is that the term indicates the gender of the individual. Aka, a trans**woman** and a cis**woman**, are both **women**. They may have a vulva or penis but that is irrelevant to their gender identities.

For those with marginalized identities, I hope that you may live your maximum life full of love, caring, and support. If you are unable to come out, be you, or transition due to concerns of safety or family, I hope you know there are those who care and support you and hope for a world where you can safely be your authentic self.

CHAPTER 4:

Partnering Styles

Monogamy & Ethical Non-Monogamy

I, like many others, grew up with the idea that love comes in a monogamous package that is ideally, forever lasting. Despite the amount of polygamy in holy books, the majority of the Western world's Judeo-Christian culture strongly believes that monogamy is the only ethical and acceptable way to live. From around the age of 19, I have struggled with the idea of monogamy. I have been in love and even considered settling down but all the while did not feel it made sense to have sex and be in a relationship with only one person. I am vehemently against cheating as it goes against my personal moral code and therefore practiced monogamy until around age 25 for the sake of my romantic partners for whom it was important. I felt that there must be ethical ways to engage in non-monogamy while still being in love but didn't know what that looked like.

In July 2016 I was walking through the streets of New Orleans after speaking at a conference for sex workers and their allies when I found my answer. My unofficial tour guide stopped when he saw friends of his who were currently engaged in a short-term triad. Though the three people were significantly older than me, I found the youngest, Daniel, attractive. I exchanged information with him and we developed a part-time long-distance relationship with monthly meet-ups. Daniel was the first person to introduce me to the idea of polyamory. A couple

> A triad refers to three people who are in a sexual and/or romantic relationship with one another.

of friends of mine also suggested I read *Sex at Dawn: How We Mate, Why We Stray, and What it Means for Modern Relationships* by Christopher Ryan and Cacilda Jetha, which helped me recognize that not only was I not alone, but perhaps there were many others like me. Since then, I now introduce myself as poly/non-monogamous to those I meet so that they can decide freely whether to consider entering in a relationship with me. Like my values and social identities, being polyamorous is a part of me.

Just like in monogamy, the key to ethical polyamory/non-monogamy is communication. Partners in all relationships can become jealous, feel under prioritized, or even just get bored. This is true for platonic friendships, monogamous relationships, and polyamorous ones. However, the constant checking-in and communication expected when engaging in ethical polyamory is greater than with other relationships. Boundaries and rules may change as the relationship continues and check-ins keep everyone on the same page.

Just as it is important to know yourself and your sexual identity, it's important to know about your partnering identity. Some people are truly happy as serial monogamists, others prefer non-monogamy until they find someone they feel is worth being monogamous for, and still others are polyamorous for life and will always have multiple loving partners. If you are honest about who you are, conversations should be smoother. Let's look at some examples of current trends and partnering styles to see where you fit.

Hook-Up Culture and Casual Sex

There is currently a strong hook-up culture that is further fed by media. People engage in "no strings attached sex" or "friends with benefits" scenarios all the time and though it can be great for some, others end up experiencing unplanned and possibly unwanted emotions and attachments to their sexual partners. It is unrealistic to expect a person for whom sex creates a strong emotional connection to be able to engage in casual sex without developing such feelings just because there is a culture of casual sex. It is also unhealthy mentally and emotionally to convince yourself you are happy with a situation that does not work for you. If you are a serial monogamist, be clear about your needs not only with yourself but also with potential partners. You might be worried about "scaring off" potential partners but if someone is interested in the same partnering style as you, they will let you know and if they're not, you'll avoid dating people who don't want what you want.

Serial Monogamy

This is the most socially accepted form of a relationship in the US. People will date for a time and then decide that they are committed to dating only one another until the relationship ends, if it ever does. Though this is generally called monogamy, true monogamy is having one partner for life. Some individuals, particularly those in arranged or forced marriages, have this experience, but many people who practice monogamy date multiple people before choosing a life partner.

There are many ways in which serially monogamous dating occurs. For some individuals, they are committed to monogamy from the start and once the first date occurs, will not date anyone else until the relationship is deemed over. Other serial monogamists might date multiple people, engage in sex, have consistent communication with all potential partners, etc., until there is an explicit verbal agreement about monogamous commitment. If you are interested in serial monogamy, either of these approaches, or anything in between, might work for you but make sure you're communicating! It can be an issue if you and your partner do not communicate your partnering styles or intentionally use silence to withhold information that would be important for the other person(s) to know.

Polyamory

The word polyamory combines a Greek prefix, "poly" which means "many" or "multi" with the Latin word for love "amor." Essentially, it means many or multiple loves. Poly is unique in that partners have agreed that each can engage in multiple relationships, whether committed or casual. At its core, polyamory rests on two beliefs: (1) that there is abundance of love to share and, (2) that no one human can provide all that you need from a romantic life partnership. For those outside of the poly world, it can be difficult to comprehend that the second point accepts having multiple and simultaneous romantic and sexual partners.

> Polyamory should not be confused with polygamy. Polygamy is a practice of an individual having multiple spouses. Within polyamorous relationships, the expectation is that all those involved can date multiple people, rather than having multiple people tied to just one partner, as with polygamy. Polyamory therefore involves a different power structure.

Possibly the most important thing to note about polyamory is that everyone, with the possible exception of one-night stands and other very intentionally short trysts, is aware of the situation. Those who engage in these relationships without the knowledge of their partners are cheating which is not considered ethical by unwritten and written poly codes.

Types of Polyamory

Like with monogamy, everyone practices polyamory differently and it's important to communicate your needs and parameters for different relationships.

Hierarchical

Hierarchical polyamory is characterized by having a main or primary partner as well as additional relationships which may take on different places (secondary, tertiary, etc.) in your life.

Example of primary with secondary and tertiary: Taylor has a spouse, a girlfriend, and a fuckboy. Taylor and the spouse may have children and shared a home. They are best friends who are in love with each other and are committed to building the rest of their lives together. They are both poly and engage in multiple outside relationships. Taylor's girlfriend may be an adventurous individual with whom they try out new foods, explore neighborhoods, and do adrenaline-based activities. The fuckboy may be the person with whom Taylor experiments sexually or simply, someone very good in bed that enjoys Taylor sexually as well. The girlfriend and fuckboy could remain permanent but may also change over time. Like with monogamous relationships, it's possible Taylor and their primary will stay together indefinitely, or they could separate if their relationship no longer makes sense.

Example of an open relationship: Ariel and Jules are in a committed relationship. They both travel a lot for work and pleasure. Sometimes they travel together and sometimes separately. They agreed that when traveling separately, they can sleep with people they meet along the way. Eventually, they also decided that for the places that they frequently travel, they can each have part-time partners. Ariel and Jules made decisions based upon their comfort levels. As their comfort with one another grew, they chose to expand their rules of engagement with one another and other partners.

Minor spoiler alert: On the TV show *Insecure*, Dro tells his childhood friend Molly that he and his wife have an open relationship. Dro and Molly sleep together for a while but Molly has a difficult time with the concept and ultimately feels uncomfortable. From what is seen on screen, it doesn't appear that Dro and Molly have conversations around boundaries and expectations which may be part of what causes Molly's discomfort.

Triads/Quads

Triads often occur when a couple decides to open their partnership through the addition of a third person, often referred to as a unicorn. The couple may be looking for a one-night stand threesome, regular threesomes with the same individual, or to create a long-lasting and loving relationship.

Just as with the other relationship styles, rules of engagement are set by those involved. A couple bringing in a third will likely continue to engage in sex as a couple, inviting the third only for play with both of them. If the couple becomes a true triad, then they may all decide to only have sex as a group of three or they may choose to have sex in any combination of two as well.

The 2008 film, *Vicky Cristina Barcelona* is an example of two friends who meet a man and begin a triad rather than the common couple seeking a third scenario.

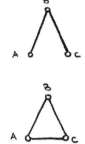

The first triangle has one person (B) who has sex with two people, A & C, though they don't have sex with each other. The second triangle represents three people who have sex with each other, A, B, & C.

Quads are often formed by two couples who choose to have sex with one another. Like with triads, there would be a discussion about who can sleep with whom as shown in the diagram. Both Triads and Quads can be polyfidelic (PF) relationships. This means that the people involved only have sex with one another. There are also triads and quads where people aren't polyfidelic (Non-PF). For example, swingers are often temporary quads with the intention of creating sexual excitement in one's married life. These are rarely about developing meaningful relationships with each of the members. The four images below are examples of PF Quads with an example of a Non-PF Triad on the next page.

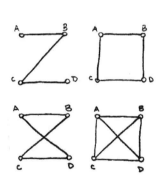

The first foursome shows that A only has sex with B, B has sex with A & C, and so forth. The second shows that A has sex with B & D, but not C while C has sex with B & D, too. This might occur when there is a mixture of straight and queer people in a foursome where the straight people of the same gender do not have sex with each other. The third is like the second and the fourth is an example where everyone has sex with everyone

Unlike the last 6 examples which assume the only partners involved are those listed (A, B, & C for the Triad and A, B, C, & D for the Quad), the diagram to the right represents a Non-PF Triad. 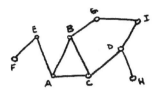 *A, B, & C may have a sexual relationship between the three of them, but C is also having sex with D, A with E, and B with G. Then those partners also have other partners and so on.*

Relationship Anarchy

Relationship anarchists reject society's classifications of relationships within a hierarchy. They do not rate or determine importance based upon relationship length, familial ties, or sexual nature. Each individual relationship has its importance and role and is not meant to be compared to the others.

For those interested in learning more about relationship anarchy, look up Andie Nordgren's *the short instructional manifesto for relationship anarchy.*

Solo Poly

Solo polyamorists consider the relationship they have with themselves to be their primary relationship. Those who identify this way can still have deep and caring relationships with others. They may, however, choose to live alone and without establishing permanent ties.

Personal Narrative

"But I Could Never Be Poly."

By Ameris Poquette

I hear this statement a lot, mostly right after I've asserted my own relationship preference, as if my profession comes with an attempt at conversion. Most monogamous people I talk to about poly insist on telling me all of the challenges that come with my relationship structure. Challenges I am intimately familiar with, believe me.

There seems to be a misconception that there isn't room for jealousy in a poly relationship. And in a way this is true, because there isn't room for jealous actions. But what you feel, and how you handle those feelings, are two different things. The truth is, that most of us feel something resembling jealousy, inadequacy, or insecurity fairly often. I say "most of us," because I don't think I've ever talked to a polyamorous person who has not expressed feeling these things at one point or another. Not feeling these things is not the definition of poly, but learning to communicate them and work through them is.

Deciding to pursue non-monogamy is signing up for a lot of work, most of which is internal. I spend a lot of my time talking to my partners about how I'm feeling, how they're feeling, how to navigate situations, potential problems that could come up and how we could handle them. The result, however, is that I am intimately familiar with my own emotional landscape, my past and how it relates to my relationships, and my (and my partner's) emotional triggers in a way that I never would have been if I didn't choose a lifestyle that forced me to do this work.

If this is so much effort, why do I do it? For me, non-monogamy means the kind of freedom I could never have in a monogamous relationship. I can have the abandon of singledom (when I want to), the ability to connect with people however I (and they) want to, combined with the stability of a serious, long-term relationship. I can go out and explore and have dates, and come home and tell my partner about them and share my excitement. I'm continually facing new situations that I have to figure out how to navigate, and I am consistently challenged, having to confront emotions I could easily go a lifetime avoiding.

This isn't to say I've worked through these things because of poly, though it's certainly expedited that process. Poly isn't the solution to any of my problems, but for me, it was the start of a journey. And this isn't to say poly is right for everyone, or that I think you should do it. Many live a happy, fulfilling life filled with the love of a monogamous relationship, and I think that's just as wonderful. But my reality will never be so linear, I've come to realize, and in a way I find that to be beautiful.

Reflection Questions

1. What is your initial response to Ameris' views on partnering?
2. What leads to jealous emotions and insecurity within relationships?
3. How do you handle jealous emotions? If you are partnered, how do you and your partner(s) communicate your needs, wants, and insecurities within the relationship?
4. What is your response to hierarchal polyamory? Anarchy?
5. What is your ideal romantic structure and partnering style?

I'm Monogamous or Poly, Now What?

I once matched with someone on a dating app for womxn seeking womxn and she hadn't immediately noticed that my profile states I'm non-monogamous. Once she realized, she politely told me that she respected my lifestyle but that she wasn't down for it so we amicably parted. It was simple and clear.

A while later I receive a call from this same young woman seeking advice. We had never met but I was one of the first people she had communicated with upon arriving in NYC and she was experiencing dating problems. She was seeking intimacy, vulnerability, and serious connection with individuals but did not require "commitment." Those she was trying to date felt she wanted too much connection for their definitions of uncommitted.

We discussed how she defined these terms. For her, commitment was monogamy and what she called, a "merging of identity." I responded that for many monogamous individuals, the level of intimacy and care she was seeking would be categorized as a "serious' relationship. Therefore, if you explicitly express a lack of interest in a committed monogamous relationship and proceed to seek out everything that is often associated with it minus the monogamy, confusion is bound to happen. I pointed out that non-monogamous dating paired with deep connections is what polyamory is about, though it didn't feel like that was what she was seeking,

I recommended identifying her needs openly with a statement like, "I am someone who feels and cares deeply and am seeking someone awesome to do that with. Commitment and monogamy optional." The first statement would let others know how she likes dating while opening a discussion about the individual ways of understanding the second statement. She decided she would be more explicit in her conversations going forward and that was the last I heard of her.

Miscommunication is common. Language is complex and inconsistent so with buzz words like monogamous, committed, casual, etc. it's easy to have a range of interpretations. So, what do you do?

1. Whatever way you identify, it's important to own it. Be comfortable knowing and expressing your needs in a

relationship. It's fine to have quick labels to describe yourself but make sure you have clear definitions for yourself of what those things mean.

2. Clearly communicate YOUR definitions with potential partners. Don't rely on having the same interpretations of overly used words. State your desires explicitly and explain what you mean whenever possible.

3. Be willing to have conversations throughout the relationship about how it is developing and whether anything has changed for those involved. It's possible your relationship began casual and has taken a turn towards committed or perhaps you recognize that you're polyamorous while in a monogamous relationship.[9] Speak to your partner(s) about any shifts. Be sure to consider how your partner will respond and what you're willing to risk and gain. Often, we are too scared to risk what we have for what we want. Sometimes we are right but often, we miss out by playing safe.

4. Be open to new possibilities. If you remain stuck in how something is supposed to look, you may miss something amazing because it comes in an unfamiliar package.

> I have a knack for deciding the ending for relationships before I've experienced the beginning. Only now am I learning how to push aside my assumptions to see where things can go.

---

[9] For those interested in specific tactics, there are internet and book-based guides for engaging in ethical polyamory and introducing it into an existing relationship.

CHAPTER 5:

Getting to Know What You Want: Yes/No/Maybe/Fantasy

Whether you're partnered long-term, engaging in a new sexual relationship, or single and want to explore yourself and what makes you tick, I highly recommend filling out a yes/no/maybe sheet. These can be found all over the internet and generally consist of a list of sexual acts one may perform or receive with space to check yes/no/maybe, just like the kink example I made for Chapter 2. These are not intended as contracts but rather opportunities for reflection. They provide an opportunity to (1) consider what we know we are uncomfortable with to give us the courage to say no if it arises, (2) explore our maybes and (3) enjoy our yeses. Even if you think you know what you like, it opens the opportunity for exploration because of the exhaustive nature of some of these lists. If you share the information with your partner(s), it will provide a straightforward list of ingredients for creating new and exciting sexual recipes.

What goes into your sexual recipe?

In addition to the yes/no/maybe categories, I recommend adding "fantasy" as a category if it's not already included in your list. There may be acts that turn you on when imagined, watched in porn, or read in erotica but that you don't want to experience in real life. For example, rape fantasy is common among womxn, but most people don't want to be raped. Many

rape fantasies are those in which an interaction begins coercively but ends with the individual willingly submitting to the advances of the other. Sometimes the fantasy is about the adrenaline or feeling so incredibly desired that the other person can't control themselves (which is not why actual rape occurs). For others still, engaging in rape play (a planned out and consensual scene that mimics rape) is a way to regain power lost from an actual rape by engaging in a safe and controlled scene. Therefore, if someone lists this as fantasy, a possible way to engage with it is to set up a rape scene in which the individual is not really in danger by having safe words.

For me, engaging in sex is about creating mutually enjoyable experiences. I focus on my pleasure because it is important, but I want my partner to be happy, too. I often choose partners whose pleasure is tied to mine but that doesn't mean they don't have needs. My goal is to discover what they enjoy because their pleasure is also important. When leading arousal workshops I talk about the difference between indifference and sincere discomfort. For example, generally I am not into dirty talk. I have trouble dirty talking but it doesn't feel upsetting to do it as long as I don't feel disrespected. So, I try to learn from partners who enjoy dirty talk to fulfill that sexual desire for them, as silly as I may feel. This goes back to the ground rule of "don't yuck my yum." Even if you sincerely dislike an act, that doesn't mean you should shame the person for liking it; simply let them know that it doesn't work for you and seek out ways to engage that please you both or at least don't displease either of you. Great sex can occur when you and others are perfectly synced but also when you are willing to grow and take risks for one another outside of comfort zones while still within your limits.

In the resources section, I have included the names of a couple of my favorite yes/no/maybe sheets where you can add in fantasy yourself. My favorite goes further than sex acts and includes what you want your body parts called, gender identity, safe words, and other aspects of consent that are often overlooked. Once you've filled out your list, get to exploring! If you and your partner are ready to experiment, full careful speed ahead! If not, check out Chapter 15: Variety: Education & Curiosity.

How Do You Want LOVE?

Dr. Gary Chapman developed the concept of the 5 "love languages" or ways in which we express and understand love. As with any other language, if you and your partner are speaking different ones, it can be difficult to make yourself understood and to understand what is being said. When our languages are different from that of our partners, it can cause us and our partners to feel uncared for or underappreciated. This can be avoided if we are aware of those languages because awareness allows you and your partner(s) to actively address one another's needs. The five love languages are (1) words of affirmation, (2) acts of service, (3) giving/receiving gifts, (4) quality time, and (5) physical touch.

To figure out your love languages, you can take an online quiz.[10] Once you know your own, you can speak with your partner(s) and let them know what is most meaningful for you. It's also an opportunity to discover how your partner(s) best receives love. This way, everyone involved in your relationship will feel cared for and loved.

---

[10] This quiz is heteronormative and only considers heterosexual couples in its language and setup.

***

There are so many possibilities for what we like and how we identify. Just like giving a child access to sex education does not make them sexual, learning about different sexualities doesn't change yours. Continue to explore yourself without judgment or shame!

NOTES

PART II:

COMMUNICATION & CONSENT: ONCE YOU KNOW WHAT YOU WANT

I am not naive enough to believe that everyone engaging in sexual relationships has the best intentions. While I recognize that it doesn't always happen, I believe that each individual should do their best to contribute positivity into the world. Or, at the very least, not to contribute more pain and trauma. If more of us lived our lives this way, we'd be living in a very different world. I hope that if you are reading this book, you share the values of my call to action: be part of someone's positive memories. Learn to recognize your own problematic behavior and work to fix it. If you live with this guideline in mind, consent shouldn't be a problem.

This section begins with a second tale from Ameris and her experience in an abusive relationship as well as experiences with women who did not actively seek consent.

*[**TW** – Emotional/psychological abuse, coerced sex]*

Consent Across Genders

by Ameris Poquette

As a teenager, I never questioned my sexuality - coming from a religious background, I never saw the point. So imagine my surprise when I found myself in my first serious, monogamous relationship with a woman.

At the time Alexis and I started dating, I had no context for relationships or ethical sexual practices, and therefore took everything that happened in our relationship as the "norm." Our dynamic was immediately volatile, with communication coming in the form of screaming and name-calling. At first, I made an effort to fight more efficiently, to transform our communication into something resembling a conversation. It quickly became apparent that this wouldn't work, and I resigned myself to our fights devolving consistently into, essentially, verbal abuse.

Alexis was dominant, and yet she didn't really like to be touched herself. This was primarily because of her own hangups around sexuality and her inability to work through them, but as a result, our sexual dynamic was unfulfilling for me. She felt entitled to intimacy, frequently insisting on engaging sexually, when I wasn't "in the mood." "Why won't you have sex with me?" she would yell, half-jokingly, after I'd declined her request several times. Often, I would "give in," tired of fending her off and just wanting to not talk about it anymore. This dynamic continued to spiral out of control until we finally broke up, after five years of dating.

The #metoo movement has undoubtedly changed the way we think about consent. It's started conversations our society has been dancing around for ages. And yet, the constant marginalization and objectification of womxn and womxn's bodies, combined with the empowerment of the sex positive movement, means that frequently women see their bodies as constantly objectified, and always wanted. This objectification is so constant that often, when engaging in a sexual encounter for the first time, or when they're first exploring, they forget to ask if what's happening is right for everyone.

Young men are taught about consent, and the way they should engage with women in a sexual context. Mothers are (hopefully) careful to prepare their sons for a world of toxic masculinity and male entitlement. These conversations are neglected when it comes to their daughters, and instead becomes a warning about how to deal with male dominance. In addition to this, sexual assault perpetrated by women is generally considered "less valid," and is prosecuted far less often then the same crime committed by a man. "They're weaker," seems to be the common defense of this problematic norm. "People can easily fight them off." What's missing in this

45

*sentiment is the fact that, in matters of emotional abuse, that's hardly the point. [**TW-O**]*

Since I broke up with Alexis, I've gone on to date several other women, in various contexts, discovering that my homoerotic desires were much more substantial than I ever gave them credit for. I often find myself as the "gateway lesbian" for women who are looking to explore. I'm fine with this role, and often find it fun and fulfilling. However, more than once, I've had consent boundaries crossed in this context. Generally, when a woman figures out she's made this error, she is mortified, and immediately overcorrects.

This is a matter of education, changing the way we talk about consent, and adjusting how we view sexual assault. Asking for consent is not exclusively a male responsibility and being an assault victim is not exclusively a female burden. These are conversations we need to be having with our children, of all genders, if we have any hope of shifting this societal bias.

Reflection Questions

1. *Have you had experiences in which you felt uncomfortable but weren't able to label or recognize them as problematic until later?*

2. *For many there is a journey involved in recognizing abuse because of the ways perpetrators manipulate circumstances or because of our own reticence to see ourselves as victims or survivors. Consider your definition of abuse or problematic behavior and see how you would categorize your experiences if they had happened to someone else.*

3. *Have you created situations that were problematic or uncomfortable for someone else? Have you engaged in*

abusive behavior or non-consensual sexual activity? Have you been honest with yourself about your actions?

Despite the discomfort of acknowledging such behavior, recognizing it is the only way to change it. Such behavior can result from experiencing abuse or be a manifestation of insecurity. It can also come from a lack of consideration for others or inflated egos. Whatever the cause, the behaviour is not justified. Seek out a recovery group, therapy, domestic violence rehabilitation resources, or an undoing toxic masculinity course[11] and continue working on yourself until you can be proud of how you engage in relationships.

---

[11] You do not need to be a man to perpetuate toxic masculinity. These are useful regardless of your own gender.

CHAPTER 6:

Communication Styles

Once you know who you are, it's important to find people who are compatible with you. It's cliché, and for many, quite difficult, but honesty is the best policy if safety is not a concern[12]. Everyone needs to measure their own safety in making any type of disclosure about themselves, but for me, risk is low and honesty at the start helps me avoid relationships that aren't really a match anyway. Despite being open, I still get butterflies in my stomach when I am talking with someone I like and I tell them I am polyamorous. This nervousness is not to be confused with shame. I am confident in sharing who I am, but I recognize that my way of life is not considered standard and could turn people away from continuing a relationship with me. To avoid any potential negative feelings, this is often the first thing I divulge to potential partners. If my dating and loving style are non-starters for someone, I don't want to wait and make it into a confession or a point of conflict later. Though sometimes it means the relationship ends before it begins, I have been lucky[13] that most people are willing to see where the relationship goes and are open to dating me while accepting my lifestyle.

---

[12] Due to high rates of homicide in the trans community and the fear of being fired, assaulted, and so on for those who are poly, queer, or other marginalized identities, these decisions are very personal.

[13] This is likely influenced by the fact that I live in a progressive city.

We all have different information we would like disclosed at the beginning of a relationship. I want to know about sexual health status, relationship status, and values. When I meet someone I am interested in, I ask about these topics because ultimately, it's my responsibility to seek out the knowledge I want. And it's also much less frustrating than finding out something later that I wish I'd known sooner!

Consider your conversation style and personality when deciding how to engage in an honest conversation about your needs. For those who are direct, something as simple as, "I want you to fuck me hard and fast from behind" works because it's clear and specific. For potential partners who enjoy dirty talk, this would certainly get their attention and they could reply in kind. However, sometimes, when we directly request what we like, others may decide to play along verbally when that isn't what they enjoy in practice. This can become apparent during early sexual encounters where you might expect the person to fulfil your blatantly stated needs and may be disappointed if they don't. There are several reasons that this could happen, including an interest, by the listener, in dirty talk and excitement to know what you want, but also comfort by the listener with what they already do. Their comfort with and enjoyment of their regular patterns may keep them from acting on your stated desire.

Rather than directly state my interests, as a taker, my favorite technique is to ask partners what they want to do to me. While, like in the above description, the fantasy and reality can differ, understanding their fantasy of what to do to you provides insight into what kind of partner they are. Mainly, are they a giver, a taker, or both. If they respond with something like, "I want to run my hands down your body, rip off your clothing, and stick my dick inside your dripping pussy," I might assume that sex for this person is very penetration based and that we may not sexually vibe. They want me aroused but their understanding of what leads me there is different from my own. That isn't to say this wouldn't be true or fun for me but if I am a taker asking about what you would do to me, this is not an adequate response. On the other hand, if they reply, "I'd kiss, lick, and bite my way down from your breasts to your pussy. I'd avoid your clit with my tongue, teasing you with my breath and biting your thighs, until I hear you moan with desperation and beg for release..." we'd have found a winner. The attention to detail and my pleasure would indicate that this person likely loves giving pleasure and we would make a good match. I also consider context with this question because not everyone will be a born erotica writer. It's simply a litmus test and I use the information gathered along with everything else I am learning about the person and our potential compatibility.

Some of you are reading and saying, but Yael, I love sucking dick/eating pussy or I don't care about receiving head. No problem! Change your fantasy request question to suit your sexual needs. You can say,

"[I love giving head], what do you want me to do you when we're alone?"

I put the first statement in [brackets] in case you want to leave the question broad or you just don't feel comfortable with that level of disclosure of what you like. Either way, it gives you an opportunity to hear what they like when the focus is on them. Perhaps they'll say they want you to ride them, finger fuck them, open your legs, or let them cum in your mouth. Encourage openness and don't shut them down. Some people will tell you exactly what they want and others may hold back for fear of scaring you off. **Just because someone wants something doesn't mean you have to provide it.** You are opening up a dialogue. You might learn that what they want is something you aren't ready for or don't want to do at all. That's ok.

In the dirty talk section we'll talk about how to enact fantasies without having to engage in acts that make one or more partners uncomfortable. Remember, avoid yucking someone's yum. Sexual desires vary and telling someone that what they want is wrong or gross, even if it feels that way to you, will shame them and possibly keep them from finding a partner who likes the same thing for fear of being shut down again. If you decide to continue with someone who has a fantasy that doesn't work for you, you can just let them know how much you like them (if that's the case) and what you do enjoy doing with them while gently letting them know you don't want to do **x**. This will let your (potential) partner know that you still like and respect them but **x** just isn't for you.

Name some ways that you can vet a potential partner for compatibility

_____

_____

_____

For those for whom the last couple of paragraphs were anxiety inducing, or simply unsexy, you may prefer taking your time and focusing on compatibility outside of sex or seeing where dates take you without sexual vetting. While I prefer to pre-approve my sexual partners, there is nothing wrong with diving right in as long as you feel safe and comfortable.

Verbal and Non-Verbal Communication

I have hosted several consent workshops and I always give participants the opportunity to say what consent does and doesn't look like. If you are reading this book, you may have realized that there is no definitive line because our world is full of gray. One sign that has come up as demonstrating both consent and the absence of consent is silence. This has frightened me because my own unsafe and upsetting

> While many of us talk about verbal consent as a sure thing, that too is dependent upon how safe the person giving consent feels. It is possible they are, or feel they are, in a threatening situation. In that case, their verbal consent wouldn't count as consent. Additionally, there are age of consent laws in many places. Therefore, the verbal consent of a person under age is also not considered valid.

sexual encounters have happened when I've been silent and my silence was misconstrued for consent. Therefore, I stand by silence as a poor indicator of consent. I say that because what one person construes as silence could include an expansive collection of non-verbal cues that are either not recognized or worse, ignored. There is a world of difference between the absence of words in place of moans and excited giggles and the absence of words accompanied by a stiff body or uncomfortable facial expressions.

ACTIVITY

Think of times in which you felt like you were clearly expressing yourself through non-verbal communication. Were there any times in which your message was misconstrued?

_____

_____

_____

Were there times when others were hurt or surprised when you understood something differently than what they were trying to express non-verbally?

_____

_____

_____

What are some examples in which non-verbal communication seemed to work well? What did it involve (type of gestures, facial expressions, sounds, etc.)?

_____

_____

_____

Different Language Styles

Language justice speaks to the notion that there is a dominant language, that of the oppressor, and other languages that belong to the oppressed. The oppressed persons must learn the oppressor's language to succeed in their world, but the reversal is not required. This idea can be adapted by the idea of their being gendered forms of communication. I won't go into detail (that'll be in the full guide) but people assigned male at birth grow up with direct language and direct requests as the norm whereas people assigned female at birth are often taught to engage in non-direct language and to be fluent in reading non-verbal cues. It is often considered rude for womxn to make direct requests or statements as they are expected to include softening language. This varies but exists across many cultures in varying degrees.

Many of us were taught to understand and recognize the language of those assigned male at birth but those individuals were not taught to learn the language of those assigned female at birth because of unequal power dynamics. This is not an excuse for those who only understand one of the gendered language forms but rather a call to action. It is the responsibility of masculine people to become familiar with their lover's nonverbal language cues, regardless of gender, and that of femme people to speak up to defend themselves and request that which they seek.

CHAPTER 7:

Enthusiasm Is Key

I want to be clear here. Avoiding issues with the law is a way lower bar for consent than I am trying to set. Ensuring that your partner(s) is enthusiastically consenting to sexual acts will, of course, help to avoid charges but when engaging in sexual acts, it is my belief that everyone involved should be so eager that stopping would lead everyone to dramatically express disappointment.

Within cis-heteronormative encounters, there is an expectation that masculine people are the people who go after sex and femme people are the gatekeepers and require convincing to have sex. There are those who like to be chased and others, particularly womxn, who feel it is their duty to feign disinterest -- even when interested! Many of us are socialized this way, even when we don't identify as cis or straight. It's called a sexual script.

Everything, if properly communicated, can work but I caution against convincing people of any gender to get into bed with you. Instead let's create a culture shift and start a sexual revolution! If we begin expecting womxn to admit sexual interest rather than pretend it doesn't exist, we change the script. At first, this may lead to sexually frustrated people but these same people will learn to voice their desires once they realize that the game is changing from one of feigned disinterest to eager engagement. This shift doesn't necessarily need to eliminate "the chase" which can be about the entire experience and which partners can opt to continue by establishing safe words so that when all parties CHOOSE to engage in a seemingly coercive sexual experience, anyone at any time can use a safe word if they are uncomfortable.

ACTIVITY

Write down ways you demonstrate enthusiastic consent - whether it's for sex or something else. Make a list. Rate the items on your list from most clear to least clear. Consider when and how you use each communication. Are you clearly communicating your wants and desires in situations or are you holding yourself back?

Freestyle Notes   **List**

(most) ○

○

○

○

○

(least) ○

Make a second list with signs that you are not interested in something. As before, rate the items on your list from most clear to least clear. Consider when and how you use each communication. Are you clearly communicating your boundaries to others or are you hoping others will understand unclear signs?

Freestyle Notes   **List**

(most) ○

○

○

○

○

(least) ○

Below is an example narrative in which consensual sex occurs. Circle examples of verbal consent and underline or highlight examples of non-verbal consent as you read.

Hey there, Delilah

by E.P.

I had been talking to Delilah for a few months. Her birthday was a few hours away when we decided to revisit our talk about her plans. She had none. At least, none that excited her or looked remotely different than the norm - birthday cake and sing-song tales.

I saw this as an opportunity to invite her to see me. 553.2 miles away, approximately 9 hours driving. It didn't take much convincing. We'd have cake, wine, and a fresh new memory of something different. When she arrived, we went out to the beach in my local town because I recalled her saying something about not having beaches back where she was from. And there's something about the aesthetic and ambiance of oceans and sand that makes you appreciate time well spent.

Fast forward, we're at a hotel I'd booked. We talked for a moment, getting to know each and every corner of the room we'd be sharing the night in. Then after small talk crept its way out of our breaths - we sat up on the bed and kissed.

One turned into three, just taps, lightly, then hard, subtle, slow lips finding their ways towards remembrance. Sucking hard on her bottom lip, I bit down playfully to let her know the mood I was in. Our hands danced across each other, feeling -- grasping -- pulling -- scratching. As I made my way down to where she was now dripping wet, she stopped me. "We shouldn't move this fast."

Taking her in, I agreed, "we probably shouldn't. I'll stop now if that's how you feel." And so I did. Pulling myself aside, I sat myself upwards at the edge of the bed, fixing my clothes which felt out of place. She went off to the bathroom to fix herself as well.

Within minutes she had a change of heart and took her clothes off while in the bathroom. Taking the opportunity from bathroom to bed, she jumped on me where I sat.

Everything felt so animalistic. Lifting her up from the bed, standing, holding her in my arms as she straddled her legs around me to keep her grip while draping her arms over my shoulders - we kissed again. This time, with less formalities. Unhindered. More lip biting. Teasingly I'd kiss her and pull away, allowing her to join her lips together again with mine. There were moments where I'd feel her lose her breath. Breathing back into her softly.

My clothes came off and I slid myself into her -- deep inside, penetrating her in a way I came to later understand she'd never experienced before. Laying her down on the bed, now kissing passionately, sucking, licking and marking each other. Stopping in between to breathe. She practiced arching her back and getting into rhythm with me as we spent the next hour changing our collective shapes.

Hair pulling, gasping, and pressing hard and soft against her...she erupted, came and shook. Receiving her, I felt her body begin to deeply settle. I made my way, shoved myself well into her mouth and let go myself. We kept at it for a few moments until we were both fully spent. We laid in bed then. Exchanging a small number of words. She placed her head over my heart to listen to it beat and I traced her every curve, inch by inch with my fingertips to carve into memory her beauty... until she fell asleep. I kissed her forehead shortly after holding her for a moment before I stepped outside. She'd given me the keys to her car earlier for me to drive since she was a visitor in a small town with crappy GPS.

I spent all of a quarter of an hour... listening to the radio and battling a short-sided confliction of a thought: Someday these feelings, like any others, may change.

I went back inside to see she had just gotten up. Bouncing to her feet, bubbly as ever, she went to the bathroom to wash her face and reapply lip gloss. Slipping into the night gown she'd come to make me familiar with. Staring at her figure, I fell in love with her unique feminine grace. Just about 4 years ago.

Reflection Questions

1. *What did the narrator do when Delilah asked them to stop?*

2. *What examples of verbal and nonverbal communication did you notice? What made it clear?*

3. *Where did the sexual scripts (masculine aggressor and femme gatekeeper) come up? Were their examples in which the sexual script was rejected?*

CHAPTER 8:

Boundary Making

When I host Consent and Boundary Making workshops, I stress the skill of setting boundaries outside of sex first. Part of why it is so difficult to figure out boundary making within intimate spaces is because we have long been dismissed when setting boundaries in general so we lack the skill in all aspects of our lives. It's a skill that is sacrificed in lieu of politeness and has long lasting negative effects. Have you ever seen a young child being convinced by a parent to kiss or hug a family member? Or perhaps when kids pick on one another and it is dismissed as examples of affection? This is particularly true between cis-male children as the aggressors and young cis-girls as the aggressed. These situations are often deemed harmless but we are in fact teaching young children patterns that later become part of dangerous sexual scripts. What we should be teaching our children is to value themselves and their boundaries. If someone does not respect your boundaries, then they are unlikely to be worth your while. This was a lesson I learned the hard way.

Think about your relationships with your parents, past teachers, physicians, and employers. In what ways do you healthily set boundaries and when have you been subjected to others neglecting your needs or boundaries? Have doctors intimidated you into procedures, tests, or medications you didn't want because you've felt ill-informed or incapable of knowing if the decision you wanted was the right one? Have you asked your parents repeatedly to respect the privacy of an aspect of your life but they consistently ignore that request and intrude anyway? Have you watched children begrudgingly give other kids hugs to make up at the behest of parents? These are all examples in which boundaries have been crossed and consent has not been respected. Causes range from cultural norms of respectful and polite practices to ideas around authority.

In the case of doctors and other medical professionals, it is true that they are generally more informed about medical practice but that doesn't mean you are not allowed to ask questions, perform your own research, or reject medical suggestion. I was once prescribed two rounds of antibiotics to address a positive strep test though I had not had any symptoms at any point. When the doctor prepared to prescribe a third round in response to another positive test result, I refused. I know that over usage of antibiotics is an issue and the doctor protested because untreated strep can cause heart damage. We compromised by deciding I would see a specialist about my asymptomatic tests. This agreement addressed both of our concerns and we both left feeling heard and respected.

Part of my ability to set a medical boundary in that scenario had to do with my entering the space with information about myself and my options. There is no reason not to do the same with partnered sex. As mentioned earlier, find a yes/no/maybe sheet that's right for you and consider what you are comfortable with and under what circumstances. This is especially important for those who become silent in the face of the unknown or when fearful. When you are presented with a new situation and you freeze because your mind is working, or the situation is causing you anxiety, the other person may wrongfully interpret your silence as consent. Ideally, your partner should be patiently and caringly seeking your verbal and nonverbal cues for your consent but this is often not the case. Therefore, preparing may be enough to give you the strength to audibly say no or physically represent your boundaries when challenged by a new scenario. It's basically like developing a safety plan for sexual encounters.

ACTIVITY:

Consider scenarios in which there is an unequal power dynamic (does NOT need to involve a sexual situation). How can you express when you are setting a boundary? Recruit one or two friends and act out the scenario to help you become comfortable setting boundaries.

People Involved:

Setting:

Conflict:

Boundary Setting:

Sex When You're Not Feeling It

In the introduction I specified that there is a difference between bad sex as unpleasurable and bad sex as painful or traumatic. I have experienced both with people I loved and/or cared deeply about. Because of my active libido, it was rare that I would say no to a partner that wanted to have sex. However, I am not someone who wants to have sex after a fight because I am a crier who tries to avoid crying. That's a whole other conversation. The point is, after a fight, I want to go off alone and cry or cuddle, not get my bones jumped. Unfortunately, it took me over a year to stand up and say no when one specific partner would initiate sex after a fight. I would give all sorts of nonverbal cues that I was unhappy or uncomfortable but the emotional exhaustion from trying not to cry combined with a fear that my partner would feel like a predator if stopped, kept me from resisting. I would eventually fake consent and eagerly wait for the acts to be completed so I could pretend to sleep. This was unhealthy. Part of the issue was my not taking an action to resist my partner. The other issue was my partner, who while definitely not a rapist, was also only thinking of himself and therefore not reading my cues. This goes back to the conversation around learning languages. In our culture, nonverbal language can be ignored. He did not seem to notice, or possibly care to pay attention to, my non-verbal language cues.

On the flipside, there are times I sincerely consent to sex that I'm not in the mood for, not because I feel coerced or forced, but because I know my partner desires a sexual release or physical connection and I choose to offer that. This practice is of course up for debate, especially given my definition of consent (enthusiastic) within the context of sex. If it doesn't upset me, I'm willing to have sex when under-stimulated when I am actively choosing to address my partner's desires. Sometimes, I end up having amazing orgasms when engaging and other times I eagerly await sleep time, but without the sadness of my example above. It's important to remember that partners will not always be sexually linked and whatever you decide to do about that is fine if you decide for yourself and are not pushed.

Lastly, sex when part of a business transaction is a second exception to the enthusiastic consent rule. From my understanding, within sex work consent is more about permission than about enthusiasm though there is a range of experiences. For some, sex work is empowering and freeing and so the consent may very well be enthusiastic. For others, sex work is an unavoidable means to survive due to limited choices. Consent will look different depending on the context. If the sex worker deems the situation acceptable, it can be considered consensual, even if they aren't eager to engage. However, just as with consent in other sexual settings, it can be revoked at any time. Regardless of circumstances and context, be considerate of the boundaries of others and your own.

CHAPTER 9:

Respecting Boundaries

Confirmation Bias

As humans, we are programmed to seek out information that confirms the ideas we already have in place. In doing so,

> For those who have low self-esteem or consistent self-doubt, confirmation bias plays a role in the opposite direction. It is used to support you in not trusting what you believe.

we also ignore information that doesn't fit with our preconceived notions. Because of this, we can often convince ourselves that we have found evidence supporting whatever we are seeking to support, even if it means misinterpreting that information. This is called confirmation bias. Just as in routine disagreements, this pops up in situations involving courtship and sex.

It is our duty to actively seek out information that does not support our ideas to see if we are correct. Sometimes we'll seek the easiest evidence to refute and then feel we have done our duty (strawman argument) when we have proven that information false. I challenge us all to find the strongest evidence against our ideas and then see if we are still able to dismantle the argument. My friend, Annafi Wahed, calls this the "Steelman" argument.

Jordan and Taylor Go on a Date

Let's say that Jordan really likes Taylor and they have plans to go out to dinner at a restaurant. Jordan's friends have heard that Taylor is really excited for the date as well. They have convinced Jordan that Taylor is completely into them and that this date will result in the development of a romantic relationship. If Jordan has a decent level of self-confidence, this information can plant enough of a seed in their mind that Jordan believes the statement to be true and unconsciously chooses to continue the evening with that mindset barring any serious evidence to the contrary.

Jordan arrives first, eager to see Taylor. When Taylor arrives, they smile and sit down. Jordan takes Taylor's friendliness and smile as evidence of Taylor's excitement. They begin talking and eventually the topic of sex comes up. Jordan sees that Taylor is acting coy and laughing a lot. This gets Jordan excited because now they see a possibility of sex occurring this evening. When leaving the restaurant, Jordan chooses to act on their assumptions and romantically pushes Taylor against a wall and kisses them on the mouth until Taylor shoves Jordan off them forcefully. What happened? Where did the information get crossed? Let's look at Taylor's perspective.

Taylor is excited to go on a date. It's been a while. They happily get ready while talking to their friends. Their friends are excited for Taylor and one of them tells Jordan's friend how excited Taylor is for the date. The thing is, Taylor is excited to go on a date – any date. They don't know Jordan well enough to know if they like them or not, that's what the date is for. Taylor arrives and smiles, noticing Jordan arrived first. Taylor likes punctuality and is excited that the evening is starting out well. The conversation eventually turns to sex and Taylor is caught off guard that the topic came up so quickly. They try and dodge some of the questions and laughs nervously but doesn't want Jordan to feel uncomfortable. Taylor knows that some people like to have sex right away, but Taylor isn't that way and isn't sure how to express that without offending Jordan. Taylor hasn't made up their mind yet about Jordan as they are

> This goes back to knowing yourself. If you know that you don't like to have sex early on into a relationship and that is important to you, take a stance and let the person you're with know.
>
> While it is the responsibility of everyone involved to seek active consent for everything, taking a stance creates an opportunity to set a firm boundary. If that doesn't work for the other person, then there are probably other ways in which they are not right for you.

leaving the restaurant when suddenly, Jordan forcefully shoves them against the wall and kisses Taylor. Taylor is shocked, offended, and upset. They shove Jordan off, shaking. Taylor's mind is spinning trying to figure out if they are in danger and why Jordan would think that is appropriate or if Jordan was intentionally being forceful.

Now that we've seen both Jordan and Taylor's perspectives, what happened? Where was the breakdown around communication? Jordan was so eager to have Taylor like them, that Jordan ignored Taylor's nonverbal cues while also interpreting them in a way that fit their preconceived expectation. This date likely ended poorly for both people. We can look at the examples of miscommunication one by one:

1) **Excitement for the date and what that means for each person**: Taylor was excited to go on a date and Jordan was excited to know that Taylor was excited. Jordan took Taylor's excitement as an initial indicator of Taylor's interest in Jordan.

2) **Smiling at the beginning of the date**: Taylor was being friendly, Jordan saw this as further evidence of Taylor's interest in Jordan.

3) **Dodging questions versus being coy**: What Jordan interpreted as teasing or coy was Taylor nervously attempting to avoid an uncomfortable scenario.

4) **Laughing with joy or interest versus nervously**: Misunderstood cues resulting in confusion between genuine and ingenuine laughter.

At the end of this night, there aren't many positive possibilities. At best, Taylor is unimpressed with Jordan's actions and cautious about seeing them again while Jordan remains confused but hopeful. At worst, Taylor feels violated, unsafe, and wary of being back in the dating world and is questioning having returned while Jordan feels led on by Taylor and potentially resentful after their kiss was rejected.

On the next page is one person's experience with blurred lines. I want to remind the readers that engagement with consent should not be based in what is or isn't legally allowed. The following narrative is complex and nuanced, just as life will be. If sex becomes a conquest or personal goal rather than a shared experience, we risk hurting ourselves, those around us, and future possibilities. However, when we approach consent from a place of desiring positive experiences for all involved and wanting to avoid becoming a negative, or worse, traumatic experience for another, we can avoid the following.

[TW – No clear consent]

Blurred Lines

By F. Williams

"I am not going to sleep with him." That's how I started out the night. I'd met T. the night before at a gala during a quick cross-country trip to San Francisco. He rearranged his day and drove nearly two hours to go out with me before I'd fly back to the East Coast. When he arrived at my hotel, I greeted him with a huge smile and a hug, "You came! I'm so glad you made it." He embraced me with an intimacy that felt disproportionate to our relationship. The kiss was a little too deep and the intense look in his eyes was a bit too open for me. I noticed it but I brushed it off.

The rest of the night kind of went that way. We walked around downtown San Francisco hand in hand sharing personal stories. Then we went to a lounge for appetizers and drinks. Throughout the night I kept feeling like he was a little too touchy feely. Unbeknownst to him, physical touch is one of my top two love languages so I usually enjoy affection but this was our first date, our first kiss, and the touch was too much even for me. While we sat in the lounge chairs he periodically interrupted our conversation to lean in for a kiss and at one point he caressed my pelvis area in a way that awakened me to a new erogenous zone that I didn't know I had. It was exhilarating and confusing all at the same time.

He walked me back to my hotel. As we approached the hotel lobby, I was thinking, "I have to find a way to say good night here while we're in a public place where I won't feel pressured when I make my move to end the night." I did not think he'd physically harm me, but I knew we would have sex if we went to my room and I just didn't want to. He walked right to the elevator as if assuming he'd come up with me. I was nervous. I didn't know what to say. Looking back, I didn't want to cause a scene or make the situation uncomfortable by asking him to leave.

He made it to my hotel door. I turned my back to the door, and said, "Thanks for a great night. This is where the night ends." A quick flash of rage and annoyance came to his eyes, "'This is where it ends now?' Oh, naw!" Then a softer side appeared followed by ridiculous pleas to come in. He kept kissing me. I pulled back. "I don't want to have sex and if we go inside that's what will happen. So we should say goodnight here." More immature schoolboy came. He's 45 years old. I'm 36. We both know that "just coming in to hang out" is not where this is going.

Maybe he understood "I don't want to have sex" as "I want to have sex but I shouldn't." Truly, I just wasn't that into him. I do not have an issue with sleeping with a guy on the first date, (despite my strict Christian upbringing), but I only do that when I want to, when I'm into the guy, and when I feel safe. This was not the case.

At that point, my back was against the door. I reluctantly let him into the room. I felt like it was the only way to take the pressure off the situation but I also felt like it was relinquishing to something I didn't want. Fifteen minutes later after one of the best orgasms I'd had in a while, he rolled out of my crummy hotel bed. He went to the bathroom then clumsily put on his clothes and shoes, "I really enjoyed tonight. I did not expect to enjoy you this much though. I still want to see you. I really like you and I'd like to bring you back here to visit San Francisco." My reply was dry, "Have a safe drive home tonight. I'll let you know when I get to the airport tomorrow." Or something else lame.

As the hotel door shut, I was a mess. Thoughts rushed through my mind.

What the hell just happened here?

I don't think this was rape but it did not feel good.

I don't think he intended it to go that far.

I should have said something when we were in the lobby. I saw this coming. By not saying something, I let this happen.

My behavior may have been confusing but I did say that I did not want to do this.

What was more confusing is that I enjoyed the sex. The lines of consent and coercion blurred in a way that I'm still not sure how to read this situation. I just know that I never want it to happen again. **[TW-O]**

Williams' story, especially her after thoughts, are common among those who end up in sexual circumstances without wanting to be. We reflect on our actions, the potential cues we gave off, and the ways in which we may be at fault. This leads to self-blame, shame, and guilt. While Williams did not experience any physical violence, the sense of shame and self-blame occurs across levels, even when one's life is in danger. However, as statistics show, most cases of rape or sexual assault occur with those you know and don't require physical threat. While there is no reason to label Williams' experience, we can agree that her verbal expression of non-consent was ignored. F. later explained her feelings about their interaction to T. who felt genuinely embarrassed by his behavior but the hotel experience ended the connection and trust they may have otherwise developed.

Reflection Questions

1. *Consider the fictional scenario between Taylor and Jordan and their communication breakdowns. Where were the potential non-verbal and verbal communication breakdowns in the non-fictional example between T. & F.?*

2. *Have you ever experienced feelings of confusion & shame surrounding a sexual encounter? Are there ways in which you worked to address those negative feelings?*

CHAPTER 10:

Fear to Reject & Fear of Rejection

Let me start off by saying that fear to reject and fear of rejection are not comparable fears. However, they can both play a role in how non-consensual situations occur. Fear of rejecting another can range from not wanting to hurt someone's feelings to worrying about your safety if the person gets mad or offended. Fear of rejection is more often tied to self-esteem or ideas surrounding what passionate romance may look like. Below we'll start with the lowest stakes reason to fear rejecting someone and continue from there.

1. You like the person and you fear they won't like you if you say no.

Just as there is judgment around saying yes to sexual encounters (slut-shaming), there is also judgment towards those who enter sexual relationships at a slower pace. In our hook-up culture, it can be complicated for those who require a strong emotional bond, stability, deep care, or love to engage in sex. Unfortunately, people will feel that they can either honor the way they feel OR get to keep the person they are dating through giving in to sexual advances. If you are clear about your feelings and boundaries and the other person isn't willing to wait or reconsider their own dating & sexual timelines, it may be an indication that there are other ways in which you are not compatible.

The actions of my first ex were clues to our overall incompatibility which I couldn't see because I was desperate to maintain a relationship with someone I loved. Thankfully, my abusive and toxic relationship ended, and I learned to seek a partner who respected all of my boundaries and cared for my emotional well-being. I ended up with the perfect person for me at the time. We flirted for a while before going out and when he tried to make a move on me (also in a movie theater) I stopped him and said that nothing could happen outside of my own timeline. That was the last time I had to set boundaries. He never pressured me into any form of sexual activity, was kind, gentle, and patient. When I told him that I was ready to have penetrative sex for the first time, he had us sleep on it to make sure. He was older than me and didn't want my first penis-based penetrative sexual experience to become a negative memory. **Don't wait until your boundaries have been crossed to stand up and defend them. You deserve to feel respected and safe always.**

2. You are concerned that if you stop any activity due to being upset, the person will consider themselves a rapist or predator and you don't want them to feel that way.

While valiant, there are two issues with this internal argument. First, you matter and therefore deserve to not be hurt. Second, your partner is likely also coming from a caring place and would appreciate the opportunity to not harm you. Let's consider these scenarios:

Even though sex education needs to improve in most places, many people, without even being familiar with the concept of "consensual sex", seek such interactions. Most of us don't want to cause another person harm – the education component is useful for learning HOW not to cause harm, which often isn't as obvious. For some of us, the desire not to cause harm can include being scared that stating our boundaries or revoking consent during a sexual act, could cause our partners to feel uncomfortable. Our partners may see themselves as predatory and shut down. If someone stops in the middle of a sexual act because they are upset, it may OR may not be directly related to the other person(s) involved. Sometimes, individuals experience flashbacks to traumatic events and become overwhelmed. This is rarely the fault of the person(s) with whom they are having sex but does require that the other person(s) follow the lead of the upset individual who may require space, to be held, to be assured of their safety, etc. Another possibility is that they are in fact upset by something the sexual partner(s) has done or boundaries that were not respected.

If you are the person who has stopped the act, and are able to, verbally express what you are feeling to the other person(s). Don't apologize for how you feel but do give them some insight into what happened so that, if desired, the relationship can continue and you can learn together what to avoid in future encounters.

If you find yourself in a situation where someone is stopping sexual acts because they are upset by a memory or flashback, communicate that you are offering a supportive space for them to process. The situation may also be upsetting or traumatic for you and others involved if you begin to feel a sense of guilt or shame. It is important to take care of everyone's feelings without shaming, guilting, or overriding the emotions of the person who stopped the act.

If the act was stopped because you or another partner did not respect boundaries, what occurred?

- Were you choosing to ignore a partner's cues of discomfort and lack of consent?

- Were you too engaged in your own experience to notice or perhaps care about what was occurring for the other person?

- Did you hope they would change their mind if you continued?

- Does your partner have trouble expressing their discomfort until after a situation has gone too far?

If one of the first three occurred where you did not respect someone else's boundaries due to lack of care or consideration, it's time to change that. While sex should be enjoyable for you, it shouldn't be at the expense of your partner.

If your partner(s) or you are someone who knows they have difficulty communicating their boundaries, you should all discuss ways to improve that communication immediately. Hoping negative experiences will not occur is too risky. Whether through mutually discussed non-verbal or verbal cues, there should be explicit conversations about warning signs that will help prevent traumatic occurrences. My own non-verbal signs have included a hard arm pat (which is sometimes used when sparring in martial arts), hiding my face, and physically holding someone further away whether through my arms or engaging my leg muscles. It's helpful if the cues you discuss are things that you would naturally do but that may not be perceived as signs of distress without pointing them out. That way, it's second nature for you to do them and easier for your partner to learn them.

Once some communication options are discussed it doesn't mean that only those will indicate trouble. There are an infinite number of ways someone can express themselves. Think of these initial conversations as building blocks for a shared language based in respect and care.

[TW – unwanted sex]

My Journey to Voice

I have engaged multiple times in sex that I didn't want to have because I was afraid to hurt the person who had initiated the act. In one instance, I hadn't seen the person in a long time and because I had always been ready for sex when we had dated years prior, he had assumed that when we met again, I'd be ready. Unfortunately, I was going through an emotional period and simply wasn't ready that first night. He didn't know this though and began to touch me. I froze. I was upset that we hadn't had a conversation and that we were rushing into something but also knew that he was such a good person that it wasn't intentional on his part. I didn't want to make him feel predatory so I went along. This has also happened in instances in which I was arguing with a partner and they immediately went towards make-up sex when I was struggling not to cry. It would feel like a challenge to say no as I would desperately hold on to my tears. It would also further upset me because I'd feel invisible. *[TW-O]* I couldn't understand how my partners didn't SEE me and my pain, confusion, or disinterest. This would then cause a level of resentment.

It took a conversation with a friend to make me realize that I needed to stand up and say no in these circumstances. I could explain to the partners afterwards how I was feeling but in that moment, the most important thing I could do was state my boundaries and prevent further sexual interaction until ready. This isn't to say that partners shouldn't be checking in and recognizing when someone is uncomfortable. My emotions were warranted in those situations because their momentary blindness hurt. However, I also want to take as many opportunities as I can to have control over my own sex life and *sexual interactions so I now take a stand for my own emotional well-being and comfort.*

An example of the new me arose as I have been editing this book. Though I wasn't upset with my partner, I was upset by a conversation we had just had so my emotions were running high when they initiated sex. They guided my head towards their groin and I experienced a flashback. The old me would have kept going to protect my partner's feelings. The new me didn't hide and my partner noticed a shift. I allowed myself to cry while letting my partner know what was happening. They didn't feel great in the moment but they held me and the next day we had an amazing sexual experience.

Reflection Questions

1. *How do you feel when you have sex that you didn't want to have?*

2. *How do you feel when you learn that your partner had sex with you when they didn't want to?*

3. *How can you communicate discomfort?*

4. *Are there situations in which you know that you don't want to have sex that can be communicated in advance (after a fight, being woken up for sex, after seeing certain people, etc.)*

3. This person has a level of power over you and you fear what could happen if they are angered by your rejection

There are successful relationships in which people date their employees, date with notable age differences, or date with different levels of notoriety in the community. These relationships are not in and of themselves negative. However, the potential for exploitation is raised by the circumstances. Therefore, if you are approaching someone who in some way holds less power than you, approach with an abundance of caution. As with any situation, ensure that you are kind, open, and respectful. Make it clear that rejection is an option and that it will not hinder the relationship or the person's status. If you are incapable of offering those promises, then you should not be placing someone in the position of having to accept or decline your invitation. Seek out someone over whom you do not hold power so that you can avoid placing them in an unfair and unsafe situation if they choose to reject your advances.

4. This person has threatened to take something important away from you if you do not do as they say

There are those who will threaten harm or to take away access to resources. This places individuals in a very difficult position. Risks may include threatening one's job or housing stability, guardianship or access to children, or the release of information individuals do not want known.

5. You fear this person will assault, rape, or kill you if you do not go along with their request

These last few reasons one might fear rejecting another are extreme; however, they are not necessarily rare. I began being catcalled at 10 years old. I "adapted" quickly -- walking with my middle fingers in the air and curses spewing from my mouth to the ears of the men who thought it was appropriate to hit on me. By 14, I had been followed around the neighborhood by an adult male, yelled at, honked at, and touched. My aunt noticed my response to these men and warned me to stay quiet. She warned me to stop responding and potentially inspiring them to further action. I now weigh the circumstances and determine how I want to respond given my fear that men angered by my responses may choose to attack me as a "punishment" for my rejection. Though the fault would be theirs, the consequences of their actions would be mine to bear.

The previous examples all address the "fear to reject." Below are examples of the "fear of rejection"

1. *Fear of killing the mood (better to kill the mood than become part of someone's future nightmare)*

People often ask how early on in an interaction consent should come up. My honest answer is all the time. One person asks the other on a date and must respect whatever the response is. You must all consent to the location and time unless someone has consented to a surprise. People must consent to food they are ordering because even if it is decided that one person will order, it's important to check-in and respect changes.

I am often questioned about the idea of seeking consent for a kiss. I am a "better safe than sorry" kind of person and believe verbal consent is the safest way to go. However, I also understand that not everyone feels that way. I think a good alternative example can be found in the film *Hitch* when Will Smith's character, Alex Hitchens, is training Kevin James' character, Albert Brennaman, on how to kiss

Context is important. If you've been having a conversation with a potential lover while on a date, and that person says they really love when their dates kiss them hard and catch them off-guard, that is a form of communication. This person is expressing what they enjoy and is likely asking for you to fulfill their desires. In this case, you'd go for the kiss because they already asked for you to. However, you'd want to make sure that a) this person felt like this was a date and isn't referring to something they'd want from someone else and b) make sure the mood didn't change into one in which they would no longer want that kiss they alluded to in that conversation.

women. Hitch's method is based upon non-verbal consent in which you lean in 90% so that the other partner can bridge the 10% gap and kiss you. If you don't want to kiss someone, you could decide not to bridge the 10%. This method may work for many, but given the fear of rejecting reasons listed before, including simply not wanting to embarrass the other person, you may kiss them even if you don't want to. This option is not foolproof but it's far better than just going for it and hoping the other person feels excited too.

Now that I am a consent workshop facilitator, I pay more attention to my own experiences of consent. I realized that the last four people that I have kissed, other than my primary partner, explicitly sought consent before the first kiss. Three of them said, "Should we kiss?" or "Can I kiss you?" which worked well for me. Each person clearly expressed their desire to kiss and empowered me to decide whether I'd fulfill their desire. Their seeking verbal consent in no way killed the mood. I had sex with two of those people and would have had sex with the third if I hadn't needed to leave. The fourth person said, "I guess you wouldn't want to kiss me" which I didn't feel worked as well because it created a sense of guilt.

I have heard from various people that they don't think seeking active consent, or having it sought after, is sexy. For various reasons and through different methods we have been taught to believe that consent isn't sexy when it can be a welcome addition to the intimacy of sex. Partners actively seeking consent make me feel respected and give me the opportunity to decide for myself whether I want something to occur. Sometimes, a partner seeking consent has given me the courage to make a move when I was hesitant because I wasn't sure if they wanted what I wanted. Openly discussing wants and boundaries develops trust that leads to endless possibilities. It also means you don't miss an opportunity that those involved may have wanted. If everyone is silent, too scared to make a move and too embarrassed to seek consent, everyone loses.

2. *Fear of being told no*

If you hesitate to ask someone for consent because you fear them saying no, what does that suggest about your action? Do you act without consent because you assume that even if they might have said no that the experience would be enough to change their minds? That may be true for some; there are people who rely on that push to help them explore something they may not have otherwise considered. However, for a lot of us, we would have said no because we meant it. In these instances, going for it because you fear someone will say no becomes a recipe for hurt and potential trauma. It's important to reflect on why you may choose to engage in an act when you feel your partner might not want to engage in it. This would often indicate that you are only thinking about yourself rather than thinking about yourself AND the potential partner. If you care about not harming them, even if you don't have a specific attachment to this person, then your decisions should include taking their feelings and needs into account.

Have To/Need To/Want To

I have heard statements like *I need to* or *have to* have sex. I have said it myself when feeling horny. However, I know that my desire to have sex is not in fact a need and no one is obligated to fulfill my desires. When we say we need to or have to do something, it implies a lack of choice. You don't *have* to do anything. You choose to do things when you decide that the consequences of inaction are worse than the consequences of action. If you feel a "need" to have sex, and act on it in spite of a partner's unwillingness or disinterest, you are making a choice to ignore their bodily autonomy. You are choosing that your physical "need" and the risk of not satiating it is more important than the risk of engaging in a sexual activity that might cause harm to other people. If you do not want to cause harm, you must choose to care and respect that person, regardless of your desire to have sex.

CHAPTER 11:

Gray Lines

As we know, there is no magic formula for figuring out consent. In most situations, there is a lot we can do to actively engage in enthusiastic consent, however, sometimes consent can be difficult to define. Intoxication, age, and emotional, psychological, and physical ability can all lead to challenging questions. Regardless of how challenging, these are important topics to discuss.

Consent and Intoxication

Sex educators often advise that consent is not possible when intoxicated due to an altered state of mind. As with everything, context is important. I believe that if you are new to one another, having sex when drunk or high is a big risk. Especially because so many people rely on non-verbal communication cues and neglect to check-in. We already have difficulty interpreting each other's hints and while intoxicated our interpretations and abilities to observe behaviors become less accurate.

> Checking in by saying "Is this still ok? Are you sure you're OK?" can be a bit of a mood killer depending on how you ask. You can, however, say "What do you want me to do to you?" What do you like? Where do you want me to touch you?" etc. Look for facial and physical signs of pleasure or pain, fear, confusion, exhaustion, to guide the experience as well.

There is no generalizable maximum drink rule as every individual responds to alcohol differently. I begin singing halfway into my glass of sangria whereas someone else may drink 6 shots and appear sober. There is a difference between being drunk and being relaxed as a result of using a substance – this is a difference that ends up being determined by those involved. If there is any question about ability to give consent, wait until a time in which you know everyone can make those kinds of decisions. If you do choose to engage in sex, be sure to check-in regularly in case anyone involved has changed their mind.

If you're already in a relationship and sexual participants have chosen to engage in the use of alcohol or drugs to alter their sexual experience, that is a different context. As in all sexual encounters, it's important to check-in with everyone, however, if the altered state is part of the plan and everyone involved is still interested, have a blast.

Consent and Age

Age of consent laws determine age at which youth can consent to sex. In the USA, each state decides for itself and the age ranges from 16-18 years old. While the laws are generally intended to avoid sexual exploitation by an adult of a child or adolescent, there are states where the law is used to criminalize youth having sex with each other! In some states, this can include registering two 15-year-olds as sex offenders for having sex with one another.

> For anyone with young people in their lives, hoping they won't have sex is irresponsible and unrealistic. Instead, talk to them about sex in a way that is honest and prepares them to make healthy and responsible decisions.

As a sex educator with some background in child development, I find the idea of criminalizing a teenager for having sex with another teenager ridiculous. It is normal for young people to want to have sex with each other. If everyone involved feels comfortable and they are careful about protecting themselves against STI's and unwanted pregnancy, sex should not be feared.

There are other states that use "Romeo and Juliet laws" which allow for sex between teens and young adults that are close in age. States determine the acceptable age gap. Issues arise when adults that are not near youth-age have sex with youth. There are many reasons a young person would want to have sex with an adult. It might make them feel mature or cool, feel loved or wanted, or be a sign of rebellion. However, this creates an unequal power imbalance and can lead to exploitative situations. It is the adult's responsibility to ensure a sexual and romantic relationship does not occur. An adult who is genuinely interested in an adolescent who shares their feelings needs to recognize the potential future mental and emotional effects for that teen.

Power Imbalances with Disability

People often conflate physical disability with cognitive and developmental disabilities. Though often perceived as non-sexual, people with differing bodily abilities often have very healthy and active sex drives and the general guidelines around consent continue to apply.

Consent becomes more difficult to determine in the case of individuals with severe learning disabilities or who are low functioning on the autism spectrum. It is crucial that they have access to sex education to increase their ability to understand and navigate consensual sexual situations as well as to protect against abusive ones. If the individual is unable to understand the acts, risks, and potential repercussions, which can be true for those with learning disabilities that hinder their ability to understand concepts, then consent is not possible. For those on the spectrum, social cues are difficult to read which can make consent more difficult to communicate. However, if the individual can express an understanding and is not pressured to engage in an act, but rather actively chooses it, then it is important to respect their sexual autonomy.

CHAPTER 12:

Unmet Needs

This section is dedicated to orgasm and issues that arise around it. However, orgasm isn't always the goal of sexual interactions and doesn't need to be. Intimacy, vulnerability, and pleasure can all occur without orgasm. What is most important is that those involved feel satisfied with their experiences.

Sexual encounters should prioritize the pleasure of everyone involved. However, a womxn prioritizing her pleasure is still radical for some. A 2017 Huffington Post article highlighted the orgasm gap, as documented in a study conducted by Chapman University and the Kinsey Institute at Indiana University[14]. When asked if individuals usually or always orgasm, the study reported that straight men[15] orgasm 95% of the time while straight women had the lowest rate of orgasm, 65%. Interestingly, bisexual women had a rate of 66% while gay men and lesbians were close to one another at 89% and 88% respectively. The comparable rate between gay men and lesbians contradicts the idea that the orgasm gap is due to cis-women's sexual dysfunction and hints at external causes.

There are so many explanations for the orgasm gap that it's hard to know where to begin! For one, among cis-heterosexuals there is a focus on penetrative sex in which clitorises are often undervalued. Freud once claimed that a mature orgasm occurs through vaginal stimulation rather than the "infantile" clitoral

---

[14] Hatch, J. (2017, February 22). Straight Women Are Having Fewer Orgasms Than Everyone Else. Retrieved from https://www.huffingtonpost.com/entry/straight-women-are-having-fewer-orgasms-than-everyone-else_us_58ac4be7e4b0a855d1d9c834

[15] I was unable to find whether this study was limited to cis-individuals or also included transpeople and nonbinary individuals.

stimulation. This contributed to developing a hierarchy in which vaginal orgasms, which are less common, were superior. Bullshit. Most people with vulvas can orgasm through clitoral stimulation and should be proud of their body's ability to give them that kind of pleasure. Whether clitoral or vaginal, orgasms should be celebrated, not ranked.

It is not uncommon for individuals to have anxiety about the amount of time it takes them to orgasm. For people with penises there is anxiety about orgasming too soon and for people with vulvas, for taking too long. The embarrassment of orgasming too soon may cause some people with penises, particularly cis-straight men to rush everything or move on quickly from sex. The concern about taking too long can lead people with vulvas, particularly cis-straight women to fake orgasms or simply decide that their orgasm isn't worth achieving. Men who have sex with women reported their partners achieving orgasm at higher rates than women who have sex with men reported achieving orgasm – theoretically these numbers would be the same, that they're not points to a problem.[16]

There is some mystery surrounding knowing whether people with vulvas have achieved orgasm, so a partner may assume their partner came when they haven't. People of all genders fake orgasms for multiple reasons but for those with vulvas, it can be easier to fake within a sexual interaction because, unless we are squirting, our ejaculations are often more subdued than those of people with penises. The best way to know, is to ask. Sometimes my ejaculations are powerful enough that partners are left without any doubt but when that isn't the case, I have had partners of multiple genders confirm verbally. This verbal confirmation lets me know that my partner is concerned with my orgasm and intends to keep going until I can respond yes or until I decide that I want to stop.

---

[16] Shirazi, T., Renfro, K. J., Lloyd, E., & Wallen, K. (2017). Women's Experience of Orgasm During Intercourse: Question Semantics Affect Women's Reports and Men's Estimates of Orgasm Occurrence. *Archives of Sexual Behavior, 47*(3). doi:10.1007/s10508-017-1114-2

Before I started recognizing myself as an equally important participant in sexual pleasure, I would fake an orgasm if I felt it was taking too long. I have since learned that it's unhelpful to fake because (1) I'd pressure myself to orgasm whenever it didn't occur quickly enough and as a result be less likely to have orgasms (2) it creates dishonesty in my relationships. Now, I simply state what I'm feeling. There are times when all the right actions are being taken but I don't expect to orgasm. I let my partner know that I am enjoying myself but that I do not expect to orgasm and that's OK. Perhaps due to releasing myself from the pressure of orgasming or perhaps because my primary partner always assures me that time isn't a concern, I almost always end up coming. To address orgasm gap, all partners must see the value in having everyone involved satisfied and be willing to have conversations and take time to do so.

If you are wondering how to have a conversation about unmet needs with your partner(s), there are at least two routes you can take. First, you can bring up the topic when not engaged in a sexual interaction. This can feel uncomfortable and depending on your partner, may require several interactions because people can initially feel defensive. Luckily, most partners ultimately want their partners to enjoy sex and if approached with care, will work towards that goal.

Explain what you like, what gets you most turned on, and methods for reaching orgasm. If there are things that you know turn you off, especially things your partner does, this is a good time to explain what you also don't want to occur. Share your fantasies, your yes/no/maybe sheets, and try demonstrating your own successful masturbation techniques.

The second method you can use is dirty talk while already engaging in sexual acts to guide your partner(s). This is less direct and can feel easier once practiced. Check out Chapter 16, "Dirty Talk" section for more information.

NOTES

PART III:

KNOWLEDGE & EXPLORATION

So far we've considered our identities, reflected on our preferences, learned about communication and voicing our needs, and the importance of setting and respecting boundaries. This section reviews

- Overview of basic anatomy
- Important information for a healthy sexual life
- How to explore sexuality, arousal, and vulnerability on one's own
- How to explore sexuality, arousal, and vulnerability with a partner

There are many for whom the recommended exercises will be uncomfortable. They are intended to push us past our comfort zones, so we may experience our sexual interactions fully and freely. It is still your decision whether you try them or not.

CHAPTER 13:

Bodies, Bodies, Bodies

Bodies come in many forms, shapes, colors, and sizes. This is true for genitalia as well. Traditionally typical XY individuals are assigned male at birth and have a penis, a scrotum with two testes, and a prostate. Traditionally typical XX individuals are assigned female at birth and have a vagina, fallopian tubes, uterus, clitoris, and labia. However, contrary to popular belief, it can be difficult to determine exactly who does and does not qualify as having strictly female or strictly male genitalia.

According to the Intersex Society of North America, which mostly references an article that reviewed literature from 1955 to 1998, 1 or 2 out of every 1,000 babies received surgery to normalize genitalia while 1 in 100 had bodies that differed from the "standard." While the years reviewed don't represent current literature and normalizing

> With 1/100, at what point does atypical become part of the norm?

surgery is falling out of favor in more hospitals, this still points to a decent sized population of "atypical" individuals. Even of those with traditional genitalia, the variation is amazing.

The size of one's phallus, be it a clit, penis, or another phallus ranges greatly. Labia minora can fit within the labia majora or flower out. Skin on genitalia can range in color depending on the area. Testes can be missing. Clitorises have been removed. Penises can be circumcised or with foreskin. There are countless ways these body parts can differ. Society has told us there are preferred versions of everything, but I like to think every option gets to be unique, fun, and worth discovering.

Bodily Sounds

We need to stop obsessing about the sounds that we make, both in and out of the bedroom. I am someone who desperately avoids farting during sex and in front of most people, really. I need to get over this. I'm not saying let's all start farting, it's not a turn-on for most. However, it's a common human function that we give too much power with our shame. Other bedroom sounds include the wetness of bodies, sweaty movements, stomachs digesting, vaginal queefing, and probably a lot more. Rather than feel ashamed when sounds occur, see them as opportunities to build comfort with ourselves and our partners. Laugh a little. Humor can be a great way to make an awkward situation feel more comfortable.

Vulvas, Vaginas, and Clits - Oh My!

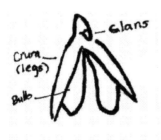

It's common to say vagina when what we mean is vulva so we are going to start with learning the different parts. Refer to the diagram to better understand where each of these parts is located.

Clitoris: Though hidden from view, clitorises are actually 4-5 inches long and shaped like a wishbone. What we commonly call the clitoris is the glans, or the tip of the clitoris. It is jam-packed with nerve endings which is why it plays such a large role in pleasure for those who have one. As the clitoris becomes aroused, the whole thing becomes erect and the areas which the legs surround, such as the labia, become sensitive as well.

Clitoral Hood: Is a piece of skin that covers the clitoris glans (tip of the clitoris) -- like a little shield. The more turned on you are, the more likely you are to see the tip of the clit poking out from below the hood, though for some, it may always poke out and for others, be always be covered.

Crura (legs) and bulbs: The crura, or clitoral legs, and the bulbs become erect as arousal grows. They surround the vaginal canal and increase sensation in the area. When I experience the arousal of this area, it is very distinct from both the clitoral glans and g-spot sensations, though they may all be connected. One theory about the mysterious G-spot is that it's the area where the bulbs and vaginal anterior wall meet. If true, it would make all three sensations directly related to the clitoris.

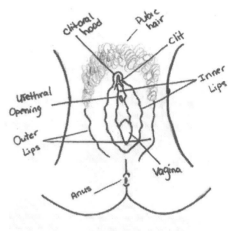

G-Spot[17]: Though not on either diagram, the G-spot refers to an area of nerves that share a lining with the bladder. It can be reached by inserting one or two fingers and massaging towards the direction of the stomach. Though not pleasurable for everyone, stimulating this area can lead to a different ejaculation and orgasm than direct clitoral stimulation. Because of its proximity to the bladder, it can cause some to feel like they need to pee as they become more and more aroused (don't worry, you aren't peeing). Because of the proximity, if you

---

[17] The "G" is shorthand for the name of the man who "discovered" the area of nerves. "Female prostate," is being used to reclaim the area, however, it's not transinclusive so back to the drawing board!

engage with a semi-full bladder, your sensations will be heightened.

Labia/lips: There is the labia majora/outer lips and the labia minora/inner lips. Labia come in different shapes, sizes, and colors. I generally avoid calling the labia the inner versus outer labia because it is not uncommon for the labia minora to protrude from the labia majora. However, that is how they are commonly known which is why the diagram uses those terms. The labia majora are where hair grows. This area can become "puffy" when aroused. Though often neglected, this is a great area to stimulate by running your fingers up and down encouraging more blood flow and sensitivity to the area.

Urethral Opening: This is where urine comes out. There is often confusion about the exiting of pee from the body of those with vulvas. To be clear, period blood, babies, and vaginal discharge come from the vaginal opening and only urine comes from the urethral opening. UTI's are caused by bacteria entering this very small canal that leads to the bladder.

Vagina: The vaginal opening, which is what you can see in the diagram, leads to the vaginal canal. This is where babies travel down and phallic shaped instruments may enter. Unlike the vulva, the vagina is inside the body. Vaginas can accommodate different sizes and shapes -- I mean, they can push out a human baby – particularly when well lubricated and relaxed. Pretty cool stuff.

Vulva: Basically, it's everything you can see. As I mentioned before, there is a lot of variety in what the lips and rest of the vulva look like person to person. For example, some people have large clitorises that can be easily seen without pulling the hood back. Others have hidden clitorises that remain below the hood and are difficult to visually find. All are normal and healthy, they just look different. Similarly, the lips can vary widely in shape, color, and size. Some people will have dark labia minora and pink labia majora, others may have the reverse, or others all one color. You may have hair that grows thick or that grows sporadic, straight or curly. Your inner lips may open like a flower and hide the outer lips when your legs are open, or everything may remain tucked inside. The urethral opening may be prominent, or it may be almost hidden. If you are not experiencing functionality problems, any number of visual variations are fine.

Vulvas don't just look different, they may also respond to stimuli differently. For functionality, you want blood (if you menstruate) and urine to have passages to leave and for the area to have sexual responsiveness if you are interested in engaging in sexual activity.

Vaginal Aesthetics, Scents, and Secretions

Though less widely discussed, people with pussies have hang-ups about their genitalia, just like people with penises do. This includes aesthetics and scent. Appearance alterations include manicuring bushes, labia surgery, and skin tone dying. Bush aesthetics have changed a lot throughout the years with current trends being towards hairless or small designed patches.

> For anyone new to shaving bushes (regardless of genitalia) who wants to start, it can cause itchy rashes and ingrown hairs so be careful about the shaving products, blades, and angles at which you shave to minimize discomfort.

Waxing, shaving, and laser hair removal are common ways to create the look you like. I support individuals in doing what makes YOU feel good. I have tried all three of these methods in the past to please partners and due to trends until I realized that what I like is a tidy but full bush.

If you have a pussy, I challenge you to love it the way it is. Most of us know that unbleached assholes are not the same color as the surrounding area, so why should you expect your different lips and the surrounding area to match. Also, get away from the idea that lips should fit or appear a certain way. If you are concerned about your own shape, check out pussy diversity art and you will see that everything counts as normal because they all look different!

Fun Fact: Pussies should smell like pussies!

Natal-vagina: one that is created during fetal development.

Neo-vagina: One that is constructed surgically.

Vaginas and vulvas have scents and are constantly creating and releasing excretions. For many who have vulvas, the scents are a sense of shame or anxiety because they worry their scents are not normal. Capitalism has benefited from that self-consciousness to produce a host of products designed to "improve" vaginal scents. These include scented sanitary napkins (pads) and tampons to cover up period scent as well as douching products which rinse out the vagina to leave it "clean." The issue is that these products can have a negative effect on natal-vaginal health. Vaginas are delicate ecosystems of their own which suffer when scented products are applied or foreign fluids are introduced to its system. These disruptions can throw off the PH balance of the vagina and lead to issues including yeast infections.

If you are a person who menstruates, it is helpful to monitor your discharge production throughout your cycle. You'll find that sometimes your discharge is lighter or heavier depending on where you are in your cycle. You may also find that certain foods influence your discharge production, texture, or scent. If you are concerned, you can visit a gynecologist who can test for vaginal infections and let you know if anything is wrong. As someone who suffers from regular yeast infections related to sugar consumption, I monitor my sugar intake and take a probiotic pill when I am concerned that my discharge is reaching unhealthy levels.

Secretions During Arousal and Orgasm

Lube is highly underrated but there is luckily a plethora of information online. Two of the most popular types are water-based lube, because they don't stain, and silicone-based, because they don't dry up quickly. See *Resources* for more info.

Water is NOT a lubricant

Vaginal secretions during sex have caused a lot of people concern. There are those who feel their vagina doesn't work because of difficulty getting and staying wet and others who feel like their vaginas are constant rivers they wish they could regulate with a vaginal dam. Neither of these situations should be cause for alarm. In the case of vaginal dryness, lubrication can be used. Remember to check that your lubrication is compatible with any barrier methods you may be using. If you feel that there is too much vaginal secretion, a folded towel can be placed under the pelvic area of the secretion producer. If you are concerned, consult with a gynecologist for more options.

When it comes to ejaculation and orgasm, there are two types of ejaculation I emit depending on whether the stimulation is clitoral or G-spot based. Clitoral orgasm leads to a creamy and somewhat thick vaginal secretion. G-spot orgasm leads to a thin and very wet substance, often in very large amounts because you can experience G-spot orgasms repeatedly, therefore releasing more and more liquid. Though it may look like pee, this wet liquid is completely different and even exits a different hole. So, grab your towel and orgasm away shame-free because that liquid is just a sign that your body is enjoying the experience.

Penises, Scrotum, and the Prostate

Like with the vulva, I'll define the different parts that make up the phallic genitalia. I have included an illustration of an uncircumcised penis as well as a circumcised penis. Please note that when the foreskin is pulled back on an uncircumcised penis, it looks a lot like a circumcised penis, it just has extra skin scrunched up below the glans.

Uncircumcised

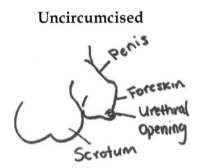

Foreskin: The retractable skin that covers the glans/head. The choice to circumcise or not circumcise is personal and often influenced by culture and/or religion. In some cases, it can be required due to an accident or because the shaft grows too large for the foreskin leading to pain. Unfortunately, most people who have been circumcised had no say because it occurs when a baby is very young. Within the medical field there have often been debates about what is considered more hygienic, more pleasurable, and a better protector against infection. If you expect to have children, this will become an important question to answer. Otherwise, if you have a partner with a penis, work with them to learn what they enjoy and how to stimulate their bodies, regardless of the presence of foreskin.

If you are circumcised, lubrication should be an important part of your masturbation routine to avoid injury. If you have your foreskin intact, lubrication is not generally necessary.

Frenulum: Is skin from the foreskin that is attached to the penis at the base of the glans/head. This sometimes gets removed during a circumcision but often the highly sensitive nerve endings remain intact. Feathery and teasing touches work well in this area that can be found on the underside of the penis.

Glans/head: This is where the highest concentration of nerve endings exists on a penis. If you are circumcised, this area is always easily visible. If you are uncircumcised, simply pull down on the foreskin to reveal this area.

Circumcised

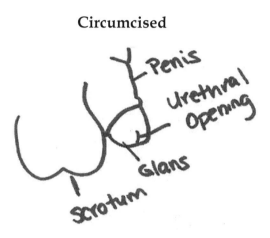

Penis: This refers to the entire phallus. There are countless names, including shaft and dick. The penis is made up of veins and erectile tissue. When aroused, blood rushes into the area leading to an erection.

Prostate: This is considered the G-spot for people with penises. It can be found by inserting a finger, or other phallic item, into the anus about 3-4 inches. For some, massaging this area can lead to orgasm without stimulating the penis.

Scrotum/ball sac: The place that houses the testes/balls (home of the sperm).

Fun fact: The testicles rise and fall with temperature changes. If the body feels cold, the testicles will rise into the body to stay warm and if warm, the balls will drop. This is to maintain ideal temperature for healthy sperm.

Funner[18] Fact: As people with penises approach orgasm, their testes will rise towards their bodies. This information can help you know how close your partner is to orgasm and gives you the opportunity to delay it. If you would like to extend your penis play, lightly tug downward on the balls so they are further from the body. This may require practice because you don't want to tug too hard causing pain (unless they like that) and for those whose balls are a big part of their arousal, a tug that is too light can send them straight to an orgasm. Consider it a fun game to figure out the correct pressure (though I recommend starting on the lighter side and moving slowly towards firm tugs).

Urethral Opening: This is where both urine and semen/ejaculation come out, though not at the same time.

Penises Comes in All Shapes and Sizes

As is commonly known, penis size, both length and girth, can be very important to those to whom those penises are attached. For those who have sex with penises, there is a variety of opinions on whether size matters.

Penises are often referred to as show-ers or growers. Show-ers are those whose penis, while flaccid, is near its full erection size. Growers are those whose size increases significantly when erect. Average erect penis length, according to a systematic review by BJU International, is between around 4.8 inches (30% percentile) and 5.5 inches (70% percentile) but that does not represent those below or above the 30 and 70

---

[18] Yes, I am fully aware this is not a word. Just go with it!

percentiles.[19] There are those who have micropenises, others who have world records for length or girth, and everyone in between. Additionally, some penises curve to the left or right. Depending upon the body of their partners, this can sometimes increase pleasure.

I would agree with my high school health teacher who said, "it's not the size of the boat but the motion of the ocean." Soon after breaking up with the person attached to the smallest penis I had fucked, I happened to sleep with someone who had a very large penis. I had really enjoyed sex with my former partner because he knew how to move to hit my angles and my vaginal walls would constrict to hold him. However, when I slept with the large penis person soon after, it felt like there was almost nothing inside of me. Despite his large size, I didn't feel pleasure nor really anything at all. He was very proud of his penis and it seems that arrogance had kept him from learning how to move and thrust in a way that created pleasurable sensations for the other person. Not everyone will feel this way but to me, size isn't everything.

More Genitalia

There is a lot of variety in genitalia across the general population, intersex individuals, and with those on hormonal treatments. For example, transmen who take hormones often experience the elongation of the clitoris into a more phallic shape. Because clitorises already become erect when aroused, so does the elongated phallus. For those who are beginning hormones, your growth will vary and may affect your

---

[19] Veale, D., Miles, S., Bramley, S., Muir, G., & Hodsoll, J. (2015, March 02). Am I normal? A systematic review and construction of nomograms for flaccid and erect penis length and circumference in up to 15 521 men. *BJU International.*

masturbation techniques. Though only very recently, there are now sex toys coming out specifically for transmen on hormonal treatment. They take into consideration not only the shape and size of the phallus but also the experience of jerking off. Opening the sex toy market helps create a shift towards inclusivity. Sex toy developers should prioritize seeking ways to create different products for the varying bodies of all sexual beings.

Anus

This is the area from which most[20] people poop. Like the clitoris or penis head, there are many sensitive nerve endings there. It can be lightly stimulated with a tongue (anal rimming) or a lubricated finger to create pleasurable sensations. I think of the anus as a second clitoris. It is amazing to have both stimulated at once! This area can be penetrated, but unlike the vagina, it does not produce its own lubrication. The walls of the rectum, the area beyond the anus, are also much thinner than the vaginal walls and are therefore at higher risk of ripping. If engaging in penetrative anal play, it is very important to use a lot of lubrication and to go very slowly. The anus must be relaxed to avoid injury. If penetrating a partner who has a vagina, you want to avoid bacteria from the anus traveling towards the urethral opening so make sure to wash anything penetrating the anus before moving towards the vagina. If penetrating someone who has a penis, this is the most direct way to stimulate the prostate.

---

[20] Except those who use a colostomy bag.

CHAPTER 14:

Sexual Health & Body Care

Sexual health is one of the few things commonly taught in sex education but knowledge on sexual health topics can vary widely. Whether you need to brush off some cobwebs, fill in some gaps, or clarify questions that were not adequately addressed in school, this brief review will help ensure you have a solid base of knowledge.

The only 100% effective way to avoid STIs is abstinence from all sexual activity as well as from sharing chapstick, drinks, etc. Even eating at a restaurant can pose a risk if the wait staff and chefs aren't careful about hygiene and/or if they become aggravated by the customer and choose to add bodily fluids to a meal. Pregnancy is only a risk between penis and vulva couples engaging in penetrative vaginal sex. With other activities, if they avoid semen near the vaginal opening, pregnancy is not a risk.

My point isn't to scare you but rather to recognize that we can only control what we can control. Our lives involve risk and it's important to know how to manage that risk without allowing our fear to control us. Below are tools and recommendations to help responsibly manage risk.

Fluid Bonding

Fluid bonding is when partners decide to have unprotected sex with one another. It literally refers to the sharing of sexual fluids, including vaginal secretions and semen. Those considering fluid bonding should make sure everyone involved has been tested recently after having waited enough time after exposure for viruses to be detected. In the case that partners test positive for anything, it's important to consult a doctor about risks for transmission. For example, there are different strains of HIV so even if all partners test positive for HIV it doesn't mean there isn't a risk in sharing fluids. If pregnancy is possible, forms of birth control should be used.

Fluid bonding is always a risk but especially outside of monogamous couples, partners in committed triads or quad, and persons who are very careful about not fluid mixing with people outside of their fluid bonded partner. Barrier contraceptives, discussed below, are key to reducing risk.

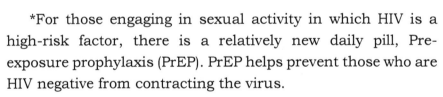

*For those engaging in sexual activity in which HIV is a high-risk factor, there is a relatively new daily pill, Pre-exposure prophylaxis (PrEP). PrEP helps prevent those who are HIV negative from contracting the virus.

Contraceptives

Contraceptives are primarily used to prevent pregnancy. Some contraceptives also protect against STI transmission while others can mediate painful menstrual cycles. Below I have divided up contraceptive methods into barrier, hormonal, and other methods. Each method has different levels of effectiveness. When searching for information about efficacy for preventing pregnancy, keep in mind that most reported percentages are referring to when the method is used correctly. Because humans make mistakes, it's a good idea to look at efficacy rates that take into account our errors to accurately understand risk.

Barrier Contraceptives that Prevent STIs

These include external and internal condoms as well as dental dams. External condoms are those that are used with a penis.[21] They come in different colors, textures, thickness, and levels of lubrication. Some condoms come with spermicide to prevent pregnancy, however, many people with vulvas have allergies to spermicide so it is not recommended. Most condoms are made of latex and protect against STIs, HIV, and pregnancy. For those allergic to latex, there are three alternatives: polyisoprene (a synthetic latex), polyurethane, and lambskin which is less effective in STI prevention.

Myth: Double wrap for extra protection.

Fact: DO NOT put on more than one condom at a time. The friction increases the risk of tearing and therefore of exposure to STIs and, if there is a vulva involved, pregnancy.

The internal condom is meant for insertion into a vagina and is made of nitrile, a synthetic latex. Finger condoms also exist and are recommended for when a finger that is being inserted into a vagina or anus has a cut and there is a risk of STI transmission.

Lastly, there are dental dams for oral sex on a vulva or anus. These act as a barrier between fluids/skin and the tongue and are made of a sheet of latex or polyurethane. Dental dams can be more difficult to find than other barrier methods. In a

---

[21] Condoms should be used with erect penises as it is difficult to roll over a flaccid one.

pinch, you can turn an external condom into a dental dam by removing the elastic ring and making one incision from the top through to the bottom, resulting in a small rectangle. These DIY dental dams are better for the anus than the vulva, due to the vulva's larger surface area. Some people use plastic wrap in lieu of dental dams but its effectiveness has not been proven.

Hormonal Contraceptives

There are numerous hormonal contraceptives with different methods of delivery. These include "the pill," taken orally and daily, the shot, taken every 3 months, the IUD which lasts 3 or 5 years depending on which type, a recent ring that can be inserted and removed by users once a month, and so on. There are two important things to remember about hormonal birth control.

1. It prevents pregnancy but NOTHING else. Hormonal birth control will not protect you from STIs.

2. Hormonal birth control can come with a host of side effects, some of which can be very serious. It is important to be in touch with a medical professional while beginning a hormonal method for the first time, or when changing to a new method, and to check-in regularly. On the other hand, hormonal birth control can be very effective in addressing symptoms of difficult and painful menstruation.

Other Contraceptives

Like hormonal birth control, other forms of contraceptives protect only against pregnancy. Most contraceptives are geared towards people with vulvas. These include the copper

IUD which lasts up to 10 years as well as contraceptives inserted before sex like the sponge and diaphragm. Vasectomies are an option for people with penises who do not wish to have children, or more children. It's a quick procedure that after a few months, will be almost 100% effective. More options will hopefully be coming out for those with penises but for now are limited to this and condoms.

Can You Trust Your Partner?

This may feel like an insulting question but if you are fluid-bonding, it's important. Can you trust your partner not to cheat on your agreements? This includes people who are monogamous having to trust that their partner is only sleeping with them or poly people having to trust that their partners are using barrier methods and asking other partners to be tested.

If maintaining your sexual health is of the utmost importance to you, as it is for many, express that to your partner EXPLICITLY. It is not enough to assume that your partner is aware of their STI status nor to assume that they will tell you if they are. Have a conversation where you discuss what you want to know. Let them know that if they break the agreements you have made to stay safe, that you want to know so you can take measures to protect yourself. Help them understand that in addition to the emotional harm they could be causing, you are also concerned about the physical harm. You can decide together or as individuals what happens if someone breaks your agreements. However, if your partner feels they must lie to keep you with them, it is less likely that they'll tell you if they've cheated or put you at risk. Encourage open communication. Now, for some this won't work. You'd drop a partner who cheats and that's completely understandable. In that case, be sure to be tested regularly so you can address any issues as they arise.

Acts and Their Risk of Infection

The information listed below references three detailed resources, two of which consider both penetrative and oral based acts and their likelihood of transmission. Where they differ, I use * for the first source[22], + for the second[23] and ^ for the third[24]. If there is no marking, it means that all sources that cover that act indicate the same information. The information is based upon engaging in unprotected sex acts. Anything that can be transmitted while using a condom or dental dam has been bolded under the "Likely or Possible" section. Remember that the most common STI symptom is no symptom so if you think you have been exposed, get tested!

Act	Likely or Possible	Unlikely/Low Risk	Does not Pass/only in theory/unknown
Kissing with tongue (only *)	Herpes	Gonorrhea, HPV, Syphilis	Chlamydia, HIV
Hand on penis or vulva (only *)		Herpes, HPV, Syphilis	Chlamydia, Gonorrhea, HIV
Fingering (hand in anus or vagina) (only *)		Herpes, HPV, Syphilis	Chlamydia, Gonorrhea, HIV (unless blood is involved)
Genital on Genital with no bodily fluids (only *)	Herpes, HPV, Syphilis		Chlamydia, Gonorrhea, HIV

[22] BC Centre for Disease Control. (2016). Know your chances.

[23] San Francisco City Clinic. (2008, June 3). STD Basics.

[24] CDC. (2017, January 04). Sexually Transmitted Diseases (STDs).

Genital on Genital with bodily fluids (only *)	Herpes, HPV, Syphilis	Chlamydia, Gonorrhea, HIV	
Sharing sex toy (without cleaning and/or using condom) (only *)	Chlamydia, Gonorrhea, Herpes, HIV, HPV, Syphilis		
Oral sex on penis	Chlamydia, Gonorrhea, Hepatitis A+ (giver), Herpes*, HPV, Syphilis	HIV (giver), Herpes+, Hepatitis B+	Hepatitis C+ Herpes (receiver)+ HPV (receiver)+
Oral Sex on vulva	Herpes*, HPV*, Syphilis*	Chlamydia*, Gonorrhea*, Herpes (giver)+, HIV (giver)*	HPV+, Gonorrhea^
Rimming	Hepatitis A+, Herpes,* HPV*, Syphilis*	Chlamydia*, Gonorrhea*	HPV+, Gonorrhea^
Penis in Vagina (only * and +)	Chlamydia, Gonorrhea, Hepatitis B+, **Herpes**, HIV, **HPV, Syphilis**		Hepatitis C+
Penis in Anus (only * and +)	Chlamydia, Gonorrhea, Hepatitis B+, **Herpes**, HIV, **HPV, Syphilis**		Hepatitis C+

NOTES

- This list does not cover all risks

- Blood, semen, vaginal and anal secretions, and breast milk are the fluids through which HIV is transmitted. Bottoming (being penetrated) during anal sex has the highest risk of HIV transmission of the sexual acts. This is due to the thin skin inside the rectum which is at a higher risk of tearing and bleeding than the vaginal wall.

- A low HIV viral load can greatly reduce risk of transmission.

Condoms and dental dams greatly reduce the risk of transmission of STIs though it is no guarantee. It is recommended that you get tests regularly if engaging in unprotected sex.

Advocating for Self

STI tests are mostly conducted through blood tests, cheek swabs, or genital swabs. You can receive exams in most medical offices and clinics, even if they send out the information to be reviewed by an outside lab. Even though performing these tests is simple, STI testing is not standard without patients self-advocating. If you would like to be tested, request a full STI and HIV test. Herpes is not always automatically included in this list so if you would like to be tested for herpes, specify that in your request.

Because the most common symptom of STIs is no symptom, regular testing is the only way to know your own status and prevent transmitting anything contracted to others. If you contract something, do not panic. Now that HIV is treatable and pap smears can detect cervical cancer early, STIs do not have to be a death sentence. Some are curable by something as simple as an antibiotic and while others are life-long diagnoses, most are treatable.

If you feel comfortable with your normal provider or gynecologist, you can be tested in their offices. If you prefer to remain anonymous, or simply unknown, seek out a clinic or unfamiliar medical providers.

Destigmatizing

While advocating for self, we can also advocate to destigmatize. There is a lot of unnecessary shame surrounding STI contraction. Herpes, for example, is treatable and if touch-based activities do not occur during an outbreak (or its pre-outbreak warning signs), transmission is uncommon. Additionally, while it can be uncomfortable for those who have it, herpes outbreaks tend to become less severe over the years. Normalizing conversations about STIs, testing, and treatment without shame or judgment are an important part of addressing the issue. Begin by discussing STI testing with partners, friends, and family members.

Preventative Testing

Having access to increasingly accurate methods for testing different aspects of health, as well as methods that allow for earlier detection, improves our ability to prevent and address problems as they arise. We are better able to prevent the development of serious issues, such as insulin dependent diabetes, when we can detect early to avoid further development through altered eating and exercise patterns. Changing behavior is often preferable to consistent pill taking or more invasive treatment.

Regular pap smears have helped me avoid illness. At one

point, I was HPV positive[25] and eventually had "precancerous cells." My gynecologist did a scrape test and was able to remove any potential malicious cells and I never developed cancer. Despite the existence of pap smears which can help avoid most cases of cervical cancer, it killed 4,115 women in the US in 2014. One chart posted by the CDC which reviewed data from 1994-2014[26], highlights the vast difference in death rates between white and black women, the latter dying more frequently of cervical cancer. There is no simple answer as to why black women die at higher rates, but potential causes include different treatment and later detection than with white women. To address late detection, information about the importance of gynecological visits and pap smears should become part of high school health education, doctors and patient advocates should be trained to prioritize addressing this and other health risks that adversely affect specific populations, and regular testing should be covered by all insurance providers. Undoing racism and bias within our society would also greatly reduce the disparity but that's easier said than done.

For people with penises, particularly those who are under 35 years old, it is recommended that they conduct testicular exams to screen for cancer. These can be done at home or with a doctor. The exam consists of checking each testicle for a pea-sized lump. People with penises should not be alarmed if one testicle is larger or one is lower than the other. If a lump is

---

[25] HPV stands for human papillomavirus and there are over 150 different viruses that are considered HPV. Warts and cancer are potential responses to contracting HPV but there are many strains that can pass through the body without leading to health problems. There is a vaccine that also protects against most of the cancer causing strains. (CDC. (2016, December 20).Human Papillomavirus (HPV).)

[26] U.S. Cancer Statistics Working Group. U.S. Cancer Statistics Data Visualizations Tool, based on November 2017 submission data (1999-2015): U.S. Department of Health and Human Services, Centers for Disease Control and Prevention and National Cancer Institute; www.cdc.gov/cancer/dataviz, June 2018.

found, a doctor should be consulted for diagnoses and potential treatment.

To Douche or Not To Douche

Vaginal douching is a process of rinsing out the vagina to clean it. There are several products used depending on the individual and can include water, vinegar, baking soda, etc.

For natal-vaginas, douching is not recommended because natal vaginas are self-cleaning (hello monthly uterine wall shedding (periods) and regular discharge)! The delicate ecosystem prefers to be undisturbed, do its thing, and maintain its own health. In the case of neo-vaginas, douching regularity is a question to discuss with your physician. Immediately after gender affirming surgery, it is important to douche because the area, as with many sites that are healing, needs to be cleaned to avoid infection or complication. Once healed, a doctor can be consulted about further vaginal health maintenance.

UTIs & Yeast Infections

Both are more common in people with vulvas than they are in people with penises, however, everyone can develop one or both.

UTIs are caused by bacteria entering the bladder through the urethra. They are more common in people with vaginas due to the shorter length of the urethra. One common way of contracting a UTI is by not peeing within a "reasonable" time after engaging in penetrative sex involving a vulva. This is because bacteria from the anus can travel towards the urinary tract and into the bladder. To avoid this, make sure to not only pee but also to have enough urine in your bladder that the stream is steady. If you pee right before sex, the pressure afterwards may not be enough to flush out the bacteria.

Whether you have a penis or a vagina, there are three things you can do to avoid a UTI:

- Wipe front to back for the same reason as peeing after sex - you don't want bacteria from the anus to travel.

- Don't hold your pee for too long because it gives bacteria time to develop in your bladder.

- Stay hydrated so your body has enough liquid to flush out bacteria.

Vaginal yeast infections are caused by the overproduction of candida, a fungus, in the vagina. The growth of candida can be caused by any number of things and my mother always told me that once you got one, it would just keep coming back. My discovery of Nutella swiftly led to my first yeast infection and my most recent infection was due to taking antibiotics. Other potential influences are taking hormonal birth control, being pregnant, the presence of diabetes, and HIV or other causes for a weakened immune system. ***Vaginal yeast infections happen in both neo and natal vaginas.***

Yeast infections often cause itchiness and/or pain by the vaginal opening or clitoral hood area. They can be accompanied by a cottage cheese like discharge, though this doesn't always occur. They can also lead to painful penetrative experiences. A gynecologist can diagnose with a sample of discharge as symptoms can mimic other vaginal infections.

Advice on how to rid oneself of a yeast infection is widely available including home remedies and pharmaceuticals, though the information isn't always reliable. It is helpful to temporarily eliminate sugar from your diet because the yeast thrives on sugar. Others suggest consuming plain Greek yogurt to support the bacteria that can help control the yeast, however, dairy can sometimes increase yeast production. Personally, I take a probiotic pill on mornings after a night of high sugar consumption or when I feel early symptoms. So far, this has been helpful with avoiding potential minor yeast infections.

Yeast infections are not considered an STI but can be spread through sexual activity. People with vulvas are at higher risk of getting a yeast infection from a partner because their vaginas are ideal environments for yeast to flourish. For those with penises, being uncircumcised can increase risk. Symptoms for a penis may include an itchy or painful rash and a thick, white discharge.

Bacterial Vaginosis

Like with a yeast infection, this occurs due to an imbalance. In this case, there is too much bacteria in the vagina. It's the most common vaginal infection for 15 - 44-year-olds. While causes are unknown, we do know such infections most commonly affect people who are sexually active and/or people who douche. Bacterial infections can also increase risk of getting STIs. Symptoms include burning and itchiness of the vagina, a fishy odor, burning while peeing, itching around the vulva, and thin white or grey discharge. As symptoms are similar to those of yeast infections and UTIs, it's important to go to a doctor for diagnoses. Sometimes an infection will go away on its own and other times you may need antibiotics. Generally, bacterial vaginosis does not spread to partners with penises but it can spread to partners with vaginas.

Vaginismus

Vaginismus is a condition in which the vaginal muscles squeeze making penetration of the vagina uncomfortable or painful. It can feel like tearing, burning, or like the penetrating item is hitting a wall. Insertion of anything can hurt, including penises, fingers, tampons, and small cotton swabs. It varies for each person as to whether it occurs all the time, sometimes, with some people, or with some objects. For some, it can make penetration feel completely impossible. Causes are unknown, but the symptoms are linked to anxiety or fear around penetration. The connection with anxiety has led to some people with vaginismus being dismissed by their doctors. One young woman who shared her story was told by her (female) gynecologist, that if she didn't deal with her vaginismus, her boyfriend would leave her.[27] Though the young woman reported this doctor and kept moving forward, others may not know what to do or may have to continue seeking doctor after doctor to find someone who recognizes and respects that they have a treatable condition. Before self-diagnosing with vaginismus, you can go to the doctor to rule out hymen-based and other issues. Be clear that the doctor should precede with extreme care.

Some physical treatment focuses on relaxing the vaginal muscles at will through practicing pelvic floor exercises, often known as Kegels[28]. These can be accompanied by beginning to insert common thin objects or specific vaginal dilators into the vagina. Individuals should take this process at their own pace. You can do this at home though it is encouraged to have a

[27] Rivas, C. (2016, November 08). What It's Like To Have Vaginismus. Retrieved from https://www.rebelcircus.com/blog/like-vaginismus/

[28] This was also named after a man which has led to a shift towards calling them pelvic floor exercises.

guided system, even if you are doing it on your own. Because vaginismus is linked with anxiety and fear, it can also be helpful to speak with a supportive counselor.

You want the pelvic floor strong because it can help you with bladder control and increase the intensity of your orgasms. If you don't know how to find the muscles, go to the bathroom, start peeing and then stop. The muscles you used to stop your stream are the same ones you want to work on squeezing to strengthen and releasing to relax. At first you may feel like the whole area is lifting with each squeeze and that's fine. As you get stronger, you'll begin to feel more specific muscle contractions. Online you can find different pelvic floor workout recommendations. For those with vaginas, there are also many items on the market that you can insert, some with varying weights, as your strength increases, to intensify the exercise. Make sure to practice squeezing AND releasing to train your vaginal walls to relax.

Erectile Dysfunction

For many, erectile dysfunction can cause a lot of anxiety. It is a condition in which people with penises are either unable to get hard or can't maintain a strong enough erection for sexual activities. Don't freak out if this happens once in a while. Alcohol, drugs, being upset or nervous, and any number of things can make it difficult to have or maintain an erection. In those cases, you can wait until the substance has worn off or you feel calmer before trying again. Freaking out or making a big deal out of the situation will only make it feel worse for those involved. There will be other opportunities for penetrative or penis-based sex. Take this opportunity to enjoy different sexual activities where an erection is not needed.

If you are in this situation, you can give each other massages to create a relaxing and sensual experience. The person who is having trouble getting an erection can play with a partner(s)' body and concentrate on them. Likewise, another partner can concentrate on creating various sensations without touching the person's penis to create new experiences.

Erectile dysfunction becomes an issue if it occurs frequently because it can be a sign of nerve damage, consistent stress or emotional upset, or a sign of another medical condition such as diabetes and heart disease. See a doctor if this is a frequent occurrence to make sure that your physical health is good. If the causes are emotional, seeing a therapist could alleviate your symptoms. There are also pills that can be taken to have an erection but seek a professional opinion first to address any potential underlying issues. Erectile dysfunction occurs more frequently in older adults and can be a sign of future cardiovascular problems when it occurs with healthy young adults.

CHAPTER 15:

Variety: Education & Curiosity

In writing this book I have had the opportunity to do research to augment my knowledge. One book on female sexuality, *For Yourself: The Fulfillment of Female Sexuality* by Dr. Lonnie Barbach, includes a multi-week program of exercises for pre-orgasmic people with vulvas. The book has a very cis-hetero perspective but the exercises can be used for anyone who has a vulva or has a partner with one. Despite being a very happily orgasmic woman, I found myself intrigued by the exercises. By reading the experiences of the women in the book, I recognized that there is so much opportunity for me to expand on my own sexuality if I take the time and have the curiosity. This chapter focuses on opportunities for just that. Whether you are a sex pro or a beginner, there are ample ways to learn more about yourself and others. You may find that some things don't interest you and that's fine. However, we often don't really know until we've tried. I challenge you to take an opportunity and a risk and engage in something you wouldn't otherwise do.

> Pre-orgasmic references those who have never orgasmed or have difficulty orgasming. Dr. Barbach believes everyone can orgasm making those who haven't pre-orgasmic rather than non-orgasmic.

Porn & Erotica

By the time I was 10, I was an avid reader. The characters and scenes moved through my mind like self-directed films. I enjoyed having the creative control that reading provided over television (though I also love TV). My love for reading eventually branched into erotica. As a young teen, I'd read romance novels to seek out sex scenes to insight the warm sensation between my thighs. It didn't take long to realize that my erotica preference involved power play, domination, and submission (though my journey towards accepting my preferences did take a while). Personalized erotica written by my partners was my favorite for letting my mind run wild.

I was never attracted to adult films because everything is already decided for you when watching porn; I couldn't control the images and scenes as with erotica. That doesn't mean I have never watched porn. In fact, I wrote this section the morning after having watched a short clip at the command of a Domme with whom I had recently began flirting. I don't think the porn itself got me excited but the command to watch it, reflect upon what I did and didn't like, and not masturbate certainly did. My point is that being willing to explore your interests in a variety of ways provides opportunities to learn something new about yourself. It may also be an opportunity to see how others engage in activities you've listed as maybe or yes on your Y/N/M/Fantasy sheets. Even if this doesn't seem like it's for you, do not discount the usefulness of identifying turn-ons and turn-offs through these mediums. If porn and erotica are really not your thing, there are MANY other ways to explore your interests.

Workshops

There are lots of workshops out there on a wide range of topics. If you live in a place like New York City, it's easy to find places to go in person. It may seem daunting to walk into sex workshops but it's important to remember that everyone else is there for similar reasons. If you don't live somewhere with ample in person workshops or if you live somewhere where everyone knows everyone, and you aren't ready for the world to know that much about you, there are also webinars. Just like regular workshops that can range from free to thousands of dollars, there is quite a range in sex webinars as well.

Workshops are great for learning anything from the right lubes to use with different sexual acts and toys to how to safely practice techniques such as rope bondage. They can make you feel more comfortable with your own questions by hearing or reading the questions of other people in your workshop. They are a space for you to recognize interests you've never given yourself the opportunity to fully explore. You may also want to sign up for YouTube channels or newsletters that vary their topics so that you are constantly exposed to new ideas. That way, you can take what you like and ignore what you don't.

*Bonus: Sex parties can serve as an opportunity to witness others engage in activities that you are curious about. This is because watching is not only acceptable at most sex parties, it is encouraged. There is no requirement to engage in anything as an attendee. Just make sure you have found a party that speaks to your kinks. There are spankee parties, daddy-baby parties, bondage, make-out, group sex, etc. There are also subgroup specific spaces across different themes such as queer, people of color, femme only, over 35 and so on.

Sites like Fetlife announce parties regularly and are a good opportunity to contact party hosts and page moderators as well as to read reviews about previous parties hosted. It's important to make sure that a party you are attending is safe and enforces strict consent rules. Before leaving for a party, create your own yes/no/maybe list for the night. You don't need to write it down but think about what your limits and boundaries will be to help you navigate a space that is new and may very well be overwhelming. Prices vary widely.

Sometimes there are pre-party "munches" where new people can meet those who attend regularly and ask questions, as well as get a large discount to the party. Munches are helpful for learning about conduct and what to expect.

How To's

There are countless books and online resources that describe different practices, positions, and opportunities for trying techniques. These are particularly useful if public workshops (or sex parties) would be an uncomfortable space for you. Like this Intro-guide, you can read on your own and decide from there. Some sex stores like Unbound send out regular emails with information and articles that normalize conversations about sex. Just remember that not all information provided is accurate so be discerning about your materials.

CHAPTER 16:

Intimacy & Vulnerability

Arousal can be an almost automatic response. Or, it can require addressing specific needs patiently and deliberately. It is not uncommon for your head to think that you want to have sex but for your body to not respond physically with readiness. It is important to be patient and loving with ourselves and respectful of our bodies. We may need to take breaks, call forward mental fantasies, use lubricants, or engage in activities that do not require specific sexual organs. Shame and self-degradation are unlikely to yield desired results.

As discussed in the previous section, communication is key. When seeking intimacy, it's important to speak to your partner about your needs and trust that they are willing to listen. Worthy partners are those who will respect your needs and boundaries. Most importantly, you must trust yourself. Trust that you know what you want, that you deserve to have your needs met, and that everyone deserves for their boundaries to be respected.

Feeling Sexy

This might seem obvious but feeling confident, sexy, and attractive is a great way to begin a sexual interaction. Some of us get a boost in self-esteem when we have sex, but, it's important to have ways to boost yourself-solo so that your self-esteem is not dependent on others. With that in mind, what makes you feel sexy? This is different for everyone. For some, the novelty of wearing lingerie, for others shaving your legs, perhaps meeting your partner without underwear, wearing boxer briefs, engaging in a texting-based power play encounter, wearing a specific dildo that brings out your masculine sexuality, and sending nudes are just a few examples. I feel incredibly sexy and confident every time I cut my hair super short because it highlights my combined masculine and feminine energy. Though my haircuts are rarely followed by sexual encounters, making myself feel sexy boosts my overall confidence.

For many, the sound of our partner's moans can be arousing because it tells us they are having a good time. Less widely acknowledged is that the sound of our own moaning can also be stimulating. If you are warming up with a partner or engaging in solo sex, try making sounds to match your stimulation. If you're just starting and feel anxious or silly, the sounds may be quiet - make them anyway. Using moans and breath work can prime your mind for the sensations you're building towards - this isn't to say you should fake sexual arousal but rather use sounds and breath as a tool to heighten sexual arousal.

Bonus: Making low pitch sounds may also release jaw tension helping the rest of your body ease into orgasm.

You can also play with breathing patterns[29] to heighten sensation by safely and consciously slowing down your breaths or making them quicker and shallow. You can choose any tempo that increases sensitivity to your genitalia and time your breaths with pelvic floor contractions. If you enjoy reminiscing about partnered sex when masturbating, try and mimic your breath patterns from those acts to make it feel more like those sessions.

---

[29] This is different from "breath control" or "breath-play" within the BDSM community which is very risky and can cause permanent brain damage or death.

Intimacy with Self

The following are activities that you can engage in on your own to build confidence and boost sexual energy. These activities are meant as suggestions so it's up to you to decide your level of engagement. I challenge you to push yourself beyond your comfort zones in a responsible manner because part of the growth process is sitting with our own discomfort. You probably know what you can handle, and this is an opportunity to see how much you can safely push.

BE NAKED If you are not already comfortable with your own nudity, take advantage of opportunities to be naked with yourself. This may include holding off on getting dressed after showers, sleeping nude, or if you live alone, walking around your home naked. The more time you spend with yourself naked, the more comfortable you'll become.

MIRRORS Take time to really look at yourself. Spend time in front of the mirror naked and think of at least three physical qualities you appreciate, or better yet, love! These can be aesthetic like the curvature of your stomach, the shape or color of your eyes, moles that make you unique, specific musculature, or anything you appreciate. They can also be functional like eyes that allow you to watch a sunset, legs that support you through a hike, or fingers that knit beautiful sweaters.

If it's still too difficult to come up with positive qualities about yourself, be they aesthetic or functional, consider the root of that. Ask yourself why you don't like a particular part of you and where that dislike comes from. Have you been taught to view your body in a certain way? How has external messaging influenced your self-perception? If there are things you know that you enjoy doing, you can also start backwards from there. For example: if you enjoy picking flowers, you can be grateful for your fingers that pluck them, your back that bends towards the flowers, your eyes for appreciating their color, and your nose for loving their scent. As you begin to appreciate how your body functions in support of you and the activities you enjoy, it will become easier to connect that with appreciation for other parts of you.

*Bonus: Given the discomfort[30] so many people experience with what they have between their legs, I recommend becoming familiar with this area as well. Some of our shame arises from a lack of exposure to our bodies or a fear that we are not "normal." We can intentionally get to know our own bodies to ease the mystery. If you are concerned that you don't look like other people, remember that everybody is unique, and on the flipside, there are always other people who are like us. While pornography may not demonstrate that, you can attend nudist events or google images to find examples of regular people.

For those with vulvas, it is helpful to grab a small mirror and become acquainted with the folds and areas that are often hidden from view. Use the guide from the anatomy section and identify where each part is on your body.

TOUCH Run your hands over your own body. What do you feel? Are there curves or ridges? Are there firm spaces creating security? Soft pillow-like retreats? Are there places you can embrace? Others too great to be held and restrained? See and feel your body, its power, its grace, and its strength.

ART Draw yourself. Recreate the lines and curves of your body or specific body parts. See the art in you. Be realistic or abstract; consider other beings in nature and how you can

---

[30] The discomfort I am referencing is different from the distress and pain experienced by those with gender dysmorphia as it is meant for those whose body shame is unrelated to their gender presentation. For those with gender dysmorphia, speak to a trusted professional or support network for resources and support in taking steps to have your body align with your gender.

relate yourself to them. Is your body like a strong, tall tree? Do you feel like the petals of a flower? Does your body become its own city? Maybe your legs remind you of a horse and its strength. Try whatever will bring you to a positive self-image.

Building Intimacy and Vulnerability with a Partner

Once we are comfortable with ourselves and have explored our own vulnerability, it becomes easier to share that with others. The process is not linear so do not become discouraged if some days you feel positive and open and others you feel negative and fear vulnerability. Life is messy and our feelings about ourselves, as well as our sense of safety within different spaces, are bound to ebb and flow. The intimacy with self exercises and the following exercises are meant to build on the positive and expand on our ability to be vulnerable with self and with others. They provide an opportunity to deepen our connections and remove barriers that may prevent us from experiencing sex and intimacy fully.

Sit Naked and Be Touched

Sometimes, whether with a new partner or old, it can be difficult for me to get into the headspace for sex – this is particularly true the first couple of times I'm with a new partner when I don't know what to expect. I also don't like to feel that sex is scheduled or expected in certain moments. It feels less natural but sex often follows going home with someone -- so I have learned methods to relax me. A method I have used to reduce nerves in new situations and to stimulate a sense of spontaneity is to ask that we talk normally but that we do it naked. I find it's particularly important for me that I be naked. This gives us time for non-sexual touch to occur which builds intimacy. When nervous, I require a slow build up towards sexual touch. Talking and nonsexual touching for

15 minutes (or as much as an hour) can build my body's anticipation so that by the time sexual touch is involved, I'm melting in their hands!

Looking and Being Looked at

Many of us were taught through TV and movies, that sex often occurs in the dark. For some of us, sex is related to darkness. It's an experience we share under the cover of shadows that envelop us. The idea of sex during the day or with the lights on can sound risqué or wrong. For others, the fear of natural or direct lighting keeps us in the dark (but my cellulite!). However, chances are, if you are having sex with someone regularly, they are already seeing you. Maybe you are exceptionally good at covering up and hiding as I used to be, but they are still sneaking peeks when they can. One way to feel sexy and increase vulnerability is to put on some light (feel free to use the ever-flattering candle light option) and undress for your partner and let them undress for you. Really look at each other and enjoy your nakedness. If your partner wants to look at your vulva, penis, or other genitalia, let them lay and stare. It's likely that they appreciate your beauty and simply want the opportunity to do so. Your willingness to be open will be part of the beauty you exude.

Fantasy Sharing

Most of the sexual world has specific preferences, thoughts, visuals, and/or acts that get them excited. Despite this, sharing our fantasies can often be a scary act. We may feel ashamed or embarrassed by what we enjoy and fear divulging that information to someone who may judge or leave us. Part of the sex worker industry is based off the need to engage in that which fulfills our fantasies within a space that can be free of judgement and free of the risk of a loved one's rejection.

Each individual should consider their own circumstances but remember that by having specific fantasies, you are not in the minority. There is a chance you are overthinking your situation and creating a space in which you feel you cannot share when your partner(s) may be interested in learning what you enjoy.

I can relate to this. Most, if not all, of my partners knew about my spanking fetish but I was often too embarrassed to state it. After a sub-par sexual session with an acquaintance, George, in Argentina, we decided to stay in touch and remain friends. Being able to have bad sex and then maintain a friendship created a trusting base. I shared with him my fantasies and fetishes and George taught me to embrace myself. He made me feel sexy, came up with erotic stories that addressed my sexual fantasies, and most importantly, didn't make me feel judged. George does not share my kinky tendencies, but he didn't have to. All I needed from him was acceptance. Since him, I have actively worked to share my interests with partners early on in a relationship. It still requires a level of vulnerability that scares me, but I have had positive experiences. Many individuals do not share my interests, but I have found that none of them have shamed me. Our being able to be open about our interests and our boundaries created opportunities for closeness.

CHAPTER 17:

Stimulation & Arousal

Regardless of what your partner's(') genitals look like, it's important to talk to them about their body to learn the best way to stimulate them so they can experience pleasure. Some people love having their balls sucked on and others can't have them touched. Some people with clits are very sensitive and prefer to be touched in the area surrounding the clit while others prefer that the clit be grabbed between the fingers. If you and your new partner(s) are exploring each other's bodies, and prefer not to state explicitly what you enjoy, explore with excited caution. Work your way up to intense pressures based upon the signals from their body. If you're willing to have a conversation, an excellent way to learn how to guide your partner is to engage in solo-sex, or masturbation, and to share what you learn. You can even masturbate in front of your partner(s) and demonstrate for them!

Myths of Solo and Toy Play

Myth 1: Too much masturbation is bad.

Just like with everything, moderation is key. We want to avoid anything that disrupts us to the point of inhibiting our daily lives. The same is true for masturbation. However, that point of daily life disruption is different for everyone. Some people masturbate once a month, others every two days, and others 5x/day. None of these are right or wrong as long as it doesn't negatively affect your life. There are even health benefits to orgasm aside from the obvious enjoyment of the sensation; masturbation can release stress and help people sleep.

Myth 2: Strong vibrators "break" clits so they can only respond to intense stimulation.

Myth 3: Masturbation desensitizes individuals making it impossible for them to orgasm with a partner.

While it can be true that individuals who rely solely on their vibrator during solo play will have increased difficulty in reaching orgasm with a partner, it's not due to the vibrator or broken clit. Some people with penises experience similar difficulty orgasming during oral sex or penetrative sex that is not fast and hard. These are both caused by masturbation techniques that are repeatedly used without varying speed, mode, and stimuli. Don't blame yourself - you found something that works, so you stick to it. If it ain't broke, right? Even if not broken though, it can affect your intimate encounters. Thankfully, the solution can be fun though it'll require patience. Start masturbating differently!

→ Do you normally lay on your back? Turn around and get on your knees with your stomach facing down.

→ Do you normally go as fast as possible? Slow down and tease yourself as you play with and touch your nipples, butt, inner thighs, labia, or balls. If you know how long it normally takes you to orgasm, challenge yourself to double or even triple that time.

Incorporate different materials and textures into your masturbation. Grab a feather and tickle yourself. Have a string of pearls or beads? You can wrap them around your shaft and lightly pull up or drag them over the vaginal opening towards the clit.

If you don't often incorporate penetration, consider using a finger, dildo, or anal plug as part of your experience.

You can also consider ways in which you can have your masturbation sessions mimic your partnered sexual encounters. That way, your body and mind will begin to associate what you do with your partner(s) with orgasm.

Myth 4: Masturbation replaces partners.

Sex begets sex and masturbation is solo-sex.

I have heard of partners of all genders talking of their insecurity about their partners masturbating. There is an assumption that if someone is masturbating it's because they are not sexually satisfied or excited by their partner. It is true that if there are sexual issues arising within a relationship, or unequal libidos, masturbation provides an opportunity to augment or address a lack of sex. However, the opposite is also true. Partners can be completely lustful for one another so that even when apart, they are thinking about each other sexually and desperately desire a release. Our bodies adjust to increased levels of sexual activity so when we are having lots of sex with our partners, our bodies may demand that we continue sexual activity regardless of their presence.

There will also be times where the object of our fantasies, or the inspiration for a masturbation session, is not our partner(s). For some, the idea that they or their partner(s) is fantasizing about another can cause distress because they think it is a precursor to cheating or a bad sign for the relationship. If you are in a monogamous relationship and you or your partner(s) are constantly thinking about a specific person that you personally know, that seems like a red flag. Another sign of a problem would be if you or your partner turn down sex with one another to instead masturbate by yourselves.

If it is difficult for you or your partner to have sex without imagining someone else, reflect on why and what may be missing from your relationship. However, passing fantasies about random individuals you've met, famous people, porn stars, the occasional guest appearance of friends, or even the random images our minds can conjure, should give you less reason to worry. Fantasizing about others doesn't automatically point to a problem. Additionally, for some, it's about what's going on in the fantasy more than about who is in it so the person can become irrelevant.

If you are still concerned about your partner's masturbatory habits, have a conversation with them. Perhaps there is something they really enjoy that you can learn to do or a fantasy you can play out. It can also serve as an opportunity to discuss your relationship.

Myth 5: Sex toys replace sexual partners.

As with masturbating, I have heard people express insecurity around the use of toys because they see them as a replacement for human beings. It is true that you can give yourself very powerful orgasms that may or may not occur in partnered sex (yet) through masturbation and sex toys. You could also cuddle with an anal plug or ask a dildo to make you breakfast but it would likely yield far less satisfying results than doing so with your partner(s). Humans can caress, nibble, kiss, play, and explore, which for many of us, are important parts of sexual experiences. Engaging with another human being or beings is not replaceable.

Rather than a threat, the use of sex toys can offer an opportunity to become closer with one's partner(s). One way is that your toys can be brought into your partnered sex spaces so that everyone involved can engage and play. This may include suggesting a vibrator during vulva-based penetrative sex so that everyone involved is more likely to orgasm during a specific act. It could be introducing a penetrative toy if not normally used for single or double penetration. Toys like anal plugs can be used for anal training that all partners engage in to bring everyone closer through the process. There are also toys for increasing sensation to specific areas, such as nipple clamps or penis rings, or for the body in general like feathers and warm wax. If introducing toys for the first time, be gentle and patient. You want your partner to know that it's an opportunity to try something new, not a criticism. Increased sexual pleasure for one or all partners will help convince an unsure partner that it's worth experimenting and learning new ways to elicit pleasure.

Another way to use toys for the purposes of increasing intimacy is to explore by yourself and act as an observer. While using different toys, think about how you and your partner can recreate experiences and sensations that you are feeling. Use it as an opportunity to have vulnerable dialogue that works towards heightened partnered sexual lives.

Keep Your Sex Toys Clean

Whether for solo or shared play, any item that meets bodily fluids should be cleaned thoroughly between uses. It is easy for bacteria to grow and can lead to problems when using the toy in the future. If you are sharing the toy with someone you use protection with, make sure to also use protection for the toy. Otherwise, fluids and their potential disease carrying agents, can pass from person to person through contact with the toy.

When choosing toys, be aware of the materials they are made from. Porous materials are more likely to spread disease. Some items can't be in contact with too much moisture. Also, be aware of shapes and how to use them. For example, when choosing anal plugs or toys for penetrative anal acts, the items MUST have an anchor. The anchor may be flat or another shape. It ensures that the toy will not travel too far past the anus. This is important because the anus leads to the rectum which leads to the intestines. It is dangerous to have anything become stuck in this region because it can continue to travel causing bodily harm.

Arousal Using the Five Senses

Many of us naturally engage multiple senses while having sex. We engage our senses regularly without recognizing it because they are part of our automatic body functions. However, there are ways to become aware of and in tune with your automatic functions to affect your experiences, just like slowing down your heart-rate to hold your breath while deep diving. The following highlights the different senses and how you can explicitly engage them and focus on what is already occurring to heighten your experiences and increase sensitivity.

Touch

For direct touch, popular erogenous zones include the genitalia, breasts, ass, and inner thighs. Though these can be fun and effective spots to hit, there is so much more of our body that can be explored and lead to arousal. As some of you already know, the skin is our largest organ. It's covered in nerve endings with different concentration levels. Aka, if you aren't stimulating the different parts of your largest organ, you're missing out. Some sensitive areas include the ears, knuckles, lower back, and neck. I have heard that the belly button and the spaces between our fingers can be stroked to stimulate the clitoris. Like with nipple stimulation, this doesn't work for everyone and can be anywhere from hyper-sensitive to a complete dud. Explore because there are different spots and pressures that work depending on the person and to learn them, you and your partner(s) must test out different areas and observe the responses.

A great way to start awakening spots you didn't realize would be excitable is to lay on your stomach or get into child's pose and have your partner run their fingers slowly around your body. It can be really exciting to add different textures and feelings to your play. For example, using a feather instead of a finger or tongue adds a light sensation. For those who are ticklish, this can be a bit of a battle of wills with your ticklish and erotic sides. Steady your breathing and concentrate on the sensation to push away the ticklish response.

Pinwheels (flat circular item with short and sharp spikes that is attached to a handle) can also serve to elicit sharp, though not painful, sensations. For those for whom pain releases endorphins and heightens sexual arousal, there are a plethora of implements one can use on the skin. Refer to the impact doll images (the dark areas are considered safest for impact play) and do your own research to understand the intensity with which you can engage in safe and consensual impact play as well as implements you can use to hit or flog an individual.

Temperature play can also be exciting, though it is important not to burn someone's skin with overly hot or cold temperatures. Ice, for many, is too intense and requires that the stimulator use the ice on their own tongue and then use the tongue as the conductor of coolness rather than using direct contact. There are different types of warming and cooling lubricants, some candles that burn at low temperatures which help avoid burns, and the use of metal objects to apply cool sensations that aren't ice-cold or wet.

Sense Deprivation

Sense deprivation is a way of restricting one or two senses to heighten the others. Normally, this includes restricting sight and/or hearing. For example, when someone is blindfolded, they begin to concentrate on sounds to determine their whereabouts. Movies model this all the time with characters who are kidnapped and blindfolded. The kidnapped person pays attention to what they hear outside or what it sounds like they are passing to determine their location. Thankfully, this phenomenon doesn't just work when we're scared, but also when we're excited.

Sight Deprivation

There are many ways to engage in sight deprivation. It can be as simple as telling someone to close their eyes (no peeking) or throwing a t-shirt over someone's face (careful to make sure they can breathe!) or it can be a little more elaborate, using a scarf, tie, or actual blindfold.

To try this out, one partner blindfolds (with consent) another partner. Then, the non-blindfolded partner(s) makes noise, walks around, or does something else that kills time. Having the blind-folded person wonder what you're doing builds anticipation and arousal. You don't want to keep them waiting too long because they may become bored, irritated, or overly nervous. Even a minute can be enough to get their minds whirring and ready to play.

Tip: If you know your partner is into impact play, this is a great opportunity to pull out different tools for impact or exaggerate the sound of removing your belt. They'll anticipate feeling an impact without the ability to predict when and where it is coming from. Regardless of your partner's preferences, they'll be eagerly trying to hear whatever you are doing.

Hearing Deprivation

Another sensory deprivation option is restricting hearing. This can work on its own, especially if the person has a strong relationship with music, but in my opinion, best accompanies sight deprivation. A simple way to restrict hearing is to use headphones. Unless you have expensive noise canceling headphones, you will likely want to connect the headphones to white noise or music you have chosen for the occasion. Like with the blindfolding, the person will try to compensate with their remaining senses which will leave their sense of touch, taste, and smell heightened. Make sure that whatever sound you use is not loud enough to harm the partner's eardrums.

Tip: Music, whether through headphones or in the room in general can be a way to bring your partner back to a specific memory or even to set the speed of your actions. As rhythmic creatures, we can move to the beat!

Taste

If anyone involved has a vulva, no sugar near the vulva, whether neo or natal.

With that being said, there are loads of flavors you can enjoy away from the vulva as well as vulva safe edible powders and sprays sold at sex stores. It can be fun to drip or drizzle flavors onto a partner, or have them dripped on you, and follow the path with a tongue. The body will feel the drip followed by the

> Make sure to be aware your partner's allergies before doing this

sensation of lips, tongue, or teeth which can stimulate different sensations. Another option is to drip flavors or place small pieces of food into a partner's mouth as they are blindfolded. The surprise of different flavors will be exciting to discern and lead to delicious kissing.

Smell

Like with hearing a particular song, smelling a specific scent can bring someone back to a past memory. There are scents that excite us, scents that relax us, and scents that disgust us. Smell can lead to powerful reactions so it's important not to choose scents that will cause a negative reaction in a partner. For example, many people love jasmine, but it makes me sneeze and I don't enjoy the fragrance. Vanilla and cinnamon are some of my favorites but too sweet for others. Find out what your partner likes. Perhaps it's your scent that gets them going. In which case, forgo a shower before sex or drop your undies or undershirt on their desk so they can smell you before seeing and touching you. If a clean version of you is what your partner likes, leave the scent of your deodorant, cologne, perfume, aftershave, or what have you on a pillow or stuffed animal to remind them of you.

Bonus: Imagination

Part of what makes sensory deprivation so exciting is that our imaginations are at work. We are unsure about what might happen and we let our minds consider different possibilities. A great way to engage in pre-foreplay is to allude to the desire to have sex at a later time or date. If you live with your partner, leaving them a sexy note on the bed, jacket, or work bag can tell them you are excited to see them later. Text messages describing what you'd like to do or with a sexy picture can also be fun. It doesn't need to be elaborate. The message serves to get the partner into a mental space for sex so that when it's time to meet, everyone is already moving towards arousal.

Dirty Talk

At a conference for sex workers and their allies in 2016, I attended a workshop on dirty talk even though I don't often like or engage with something when I feel I'm not naturally good at it. While I didn't consider dirty talk a necessary skill, the workshop was an opportunity to learn something new and to up my sexy points. I considered myself attractive, but I didn't see myself as sexy because of the specific definition I had in my head. Learning techniques from a sex worker seemed like a perfect opportunity to increase my sexiness and learn to be OK practicing something I am not good at. That workshop was probably one of the most useful workshops I've attended in my sexology career.

It was soon apparent that dirty talk didn't just have to be for my partner, it could be for me, too. Before this point, I had never found partners using dirty talk attractive but with time I have noticed a shift. If dirty talk makes you uncomfortable but you are interested in trying it out, it can be helpful to consider what you'd want to communicate and how. My main takeaways were four reasons to engage in dirty talk.

Below, I provide an explanation of the four reasons, examples, and a space for you to add your own lines. That way, you can practice alone until your statements feel natural and you are able to use them more comfortably when the opportunity arises.

To Direct Actions or Express Desires

Many of us are wary about offering direction or constructive criticism to our partners during sex for fear of making them feel inadequate. This can lead to less than amazing sex because we are missing what we need to feel pleasure or to orgasm. The workshop facilitator suggested dirty talk as a sexy way to provide instruction without having your partner feel self-conscious. This works really well if you frame the instruction around how attractive you find your partner and how you want to enjoy them or about how well they can please you.

For example:

> Baby, get on top and look at me. I want to SEE you while we fuck.
>
> Get on your hands and knees. I need to see that beautiful/sexy ass.
>
> I need to suck on that [insert body part]. You taste so good.
>
> I don't know if I can handle it if you touch my [insert body part].[31]
>
> Ohh, slow down, I want to feel everything, it feels so good.

All these statements take a positive angle and can leave your partner feeling attractive, capable, and excited to fulfill your sexual needs. What are some statements you could use?

_____

_____

_____

---

[31] This depends greatly on the context with which it is said. If said with a serious tone, do not touch. If said playfully or in a flirtatious way, it can work. If you are concerned about confusing your partner, choose a clearer line.

To Excite or Reassure Yourself

This can work in two ways. First, there may be statements you feel sexy saying, ranging from the simple to the elaborate.

Fuck me.

I want to be inside you.

You've been a bad _____ (insert gender or other identifier). You must be disciplined.

Alternatively, there may be lines that if said by your partner, would excite you or assure you of their enjoyment in your sexual encounter. These are similar to those listed above. Some additions I would make are the following:

You look sexy when you're about to cum.

(Some people feel embarrassed by their facial expressions during sex so being reassured that you/they are attractive may help you/them relax and enjoy the experience.)

I love eating your pussy/sucking your dick. I could do this for hours.

(For individuals in general but particularly for people with vulvas, there can be anxiousness around how long it takes to orgasm. Once individuals start worrying about how long they are taking, it distracts from their experience making orgasm less likely. If this is true for you or your partner, incorporate a reassuring statement that lets the receiver know that their pleasure is important and worth the work and wait.)

No one else has made me this wet/hard.

(I'm not recommending lying but if this is true, say it! It can be an incredible ego boost. If there is another compliment you can sincerely offer, do. Confidence that is validated or constructed by a partner's words can positively affect your sexual interaction.)

What are some statements you could use to excite yourself or you would like to hear your partner(s) say to you?

_____

_____

_____

To Excite Your Partner(s)

These can be the same lines said when you are exciting yourself or they may be completely different based upon what you and your partner(s) finds sexy. There are multiple ways to discover what might turn your partner on. The most obvious is to ask.

If you and your partner have filled out my favorite Yes/No/Maybe sheet, you'll have talked about what you want body parts and acts called as well as how you want to be called. For example, I don't like the term "making love" and prefer to say "fucking." I like to be called by my given name and I don't quite have a name for my vulva and vagina that I truly enjoy for dirty talk but will continue to use "pussy" until I hear something I prefer. So if my partner is trying to use dirty talk on me, they'll keep that information in mind and I will consider the names they prefer when using dirty talk on them.

Another way to discover your partner's turn-ons is observation. See how your partner responds to different situations and words and how you can use that to heighten their experience. They may also directly ask you. If you feel silly using dirty talk but your partner has asked if you will, take a chance (as long as you feel safe). What you may feel silly doing could make your partner melt with joy and pleasure.

If you have a partner or partners, what are some statements you think they'd enjoy hearing? You can even ask them to fill it out for you!

_____

_____

_____

To Create Space for Safe Fantasy Play

Dirty talk can be really effective when you do not want to engage in a specific act but do want to help a partner meet a certain need. It can also be used to safely explore something you're not quite ready for while respecting your boundaries.

At the workshop I attended, the facilitator talked about a client who wanted to engage in anal sex which is not something she offers on her dates[32]. Instead, she got into doggy style as if they were going to have anal sex and grabbed his penis with her lubricated hand. She then began talking out his fantasy, "oh, my asshole is so tight, you are stretching me..." and so forth. The client was so taken in by her words that he felt extremely satisfied by the end of the session.

If there are acts that you, or someone else you know, want to engage in and someone else does not, consider the use of dirty talk for getting closer. It can also be used to role play or experiment with fantasies you are not ready for or fearful of trying.

---

[32] "Dates" is the word used by many sex workers for sessions with clients.

What are examples of when you could use this?

_____

_____

_____

* * *

When engaging in dirty talk, consider your partner's comfort levels and how they want to be addressed. Make sure not to address them by a term or name that offends them. For a lot of people, the idea of dirty talk is overwhelming, unattractive, or unimaginable so it's important to start small. Many people have a specific idea of what dirty talk is and might be open to it if they knew more than what they've seen on porn or comedy television.

If you are concerned about their response, begin with statements or requests that you believe they'd be comfortable with and ask them afterwards how they felt. It's great if they don't even realize the statements were dirty talk ("that feels so good," "touch me there," etc.) because it may make them more willing to engage with the idea. This will open up the conversation so you can begin consensually incorporating what you'd like to do.

Lastly, if there are words you want to hear, let your partner know. As we talked about before, just because you asked doesn't mean they have to deliver. However, it's possible that they'll be interested, whether out of their own interest or to increase your excitement and pleasure, especially if you have shown interest in doing so for them.

NOTES

Conclusion

I get approached on buses, subways, and the street by complete strangers and not just for directions. Some people will tell me about their lives or someone I remind them of. It seems I have that "sort of" face. This paired with my openness to discuss sex-related topics has also meant that acquaintances and friends have felt comfortable speaking with me about their sex questions. Now that I lead public workshops, this has translated into strangers approaching me to talk about sex though I always caution that I cannot offer counseling. Conversations are limited to knowledge sharing and, most importantly, a space where individuals feel accepted and safe to discuss questions that they have, until then, been nervous about voicing. This space is vital.

Throughout this Intro-guide you have had the opportunity to reflect on yourself and to consider others in your life. You've become familiar with different sexually-related identities, gender identities, and communication styles while unpacking consent, discovering opportunities for fun exploration, and acquiring further knowledge.

I hope, after reading this book, that you are walking away with the following:

1. An acceptance of yourself and of others who may or may not share your identities.

2. An increased appreciation of consent and a renewed commitment and ability to respect boundaries.

3. An increased appreciation of consent and a renewed commitment to respect your own boundaries, as well as tools for doing so.

4. A curiosity to explore new and uncharted territory in search of positive and exciting sexual experiences.

If any of these are true, or if you feel you've gained other positive experiences from reading this Intro-guide, I urge you to bring that into the world and share it. If you feel inspired then begin by creating a space where your current or future partners feel comfortable talking – do this by withholding judgment, being open to new things, and sharing yourself. This step is just the beginning. Sex positivity is a culture in the making. It is not simply becoming comfortable and accepting of ourselves and our partners. It's a call to action to make society a welcoming, safe, and positive environment for all of us.

Part of creating that society is normalizing conversations around sex. You can start by speaking with friends and sharing sex positive and inclusive articles on social media. You could even start a small sex positive group on social media or in-person. To help stimulate the group, you can post an article, question, or tip of the week so people have something specific to respond to. In my experience, some people will come with questions and once someone is open, more are likely to follow their lead. Be honest about your own comfort levels and how you are growing in this process with everyone else. You can also ask individuals to take turns leading or facilitating the discussions. This is useful because it reduces individual burden while expanding the number of voices and experiences that are guiding a space.

I am in the process of creating an organization dedicated to the development of community-led peer sex education spaces. If you are interested in assistance creating a group in your community contact me through Facebook or Email.

Afterward

While writing this Intro-guide, there was so much I wanted to include - important background, context, history, and analysis. There are also many voices that remain unheard in these pages. I could spend the next few years adding to this and would probably still feel the same way. This Intro-guide is just that, an intro. I hope that is has opened opportunities for your personal growth, development, and pleasure. I urge you to use the vast amount of information available online, in books, through workshops, and of course personal connection and experience to get deeper into discovering yourself and your sexuality.

For those, who like me, are drawn to the sociological, I have already started working on a *Nerd's Guide to a Sex Positive You*, which goes into the history, theory, and context of some of the topics discussed here. I am also collecting sexual identity narratives to create an anthology of experiences and voices. If this Intro-guide brought up anything you would like to share, please contact me at **yaelthesexgeek@gmail.com** to learn more.

Glossary

For Sexual and Romantic Orientations, see pages 11 – 13

For Kink and BDSM related terms, see pages 18 - 21

For more Gender Identities, see pages 24 – 25

For Partnering Styles, see pages 28 – 33

For Anatomy, see pages 94 – 97; 100 – 102

Binary

Refers to circumstances in which there are two options. Within conversations of sex, it refers to the options of male and female. Within sexuality, the options of gay/lesbian and straight.

Cismen

Men whose gender identity matches their assigned sex at birth.

Ciswomen

Women whose gender identity matches their assigned sex at birth.

Consent

Outside of the contexts of sex, I define consent as permission. I say this because there are acts we choose to engage in that may not be our first choice, however, given the circumstances, it makes the most sense. However, when referencing sex, I consider consent to be an enthusiastic* agreement to engage in a specific act and a non-negotiable for healthy and positive sex. Consent is something given continuously and can therefore be revoked at any point. Consent cannot come as the result of coercion, force, or threat because then it is no longer given freely. Consent is non-negotiable. If a sexual act occurs without consent, it is, at a minimum, sexual assault.

We decide the terms of our enthusiastic consent. In my example of sometimes having sex with a partner when I feel safe but also tired, my enthusiasm is about addressing my partner's desire, not about my sexual libido. If I am giving my consent freely and openly, this also counts.

Don't yuck my yum

It's okay to not like what someone else likes but it's not okay to be rude about it. Sexuality is complex and diverse, so it makes sense that what makes one person excited might make someone else uncomfortable. However, no one else needs to hear your opinions on their sexual practices. You can politely decline a sexual act or state that you are not interested in an activity without making the other person feel ashamed.

If you are concerned that someone might be engaging in unhealthy practices that can negatively affect others, do some research before speaking with them. Stigma can influence our understanding of "healthy" and telling someone their sexuality is wrong or bad can be damaging towards their self-esteem. If you find that the practice is in fact dangerous, invite the person into a non-accusatory space to discuss.

Foreplay & Pre-Foreplay

For many, foreplay includes oral sex and hand based sexual acts. However, I consider all acts involving genitalia or the anus to be sex. For me, foreplay is about engaging the five senses without "sexual" touching (see section on arousal). Pre-Foreplay includes mental play such as sending a dirty text or leaving a sexy note with promises of something exciting to come.

Heteronormative

Examples in which heterosexual behavior is seen as normal, superior, or the assumed given.

Natal & Neo Vaginas

Natal vaginas refer to those with which people are born. Neo vaginas refer to those constructed as part of gender affirming surgery.

Orgasm

Sexual climax at a pleasurable peak that often, but not always, results in the release of fluids from the genitals.

Orgasm Gap

The orgasm gap is the unequal rate at which different groups orgasm. Heterosexual men orgasm at significantly higher rates than any other group and lesbians at much higher rates than both bisexual and straight women. This is an important topic because it speaks to cultural norms that prevent certain populations from reaching their orgasmic potential. The orgasm gap has often been blamed on the false belief that people with vulvas have an inability to orgasm.

Sex

There is no simple definition. For some, there need not be physical touch to count as sex, for example, phone sex. Personally, I define sex as any act involving genitalia or the anus. This includes penetration, oral sex, and digital (finger) stimulation that occurs between two or more people. I want to highlight that these are all EQUALLY valid forms of sex. When we see penetration as "the" form of sex, it creates a hierarchy that inherently undervalues clitoral and other forms of stimulation that may be necessary for orgasm or pleasure.

Once we start seeing sex as sex, regardless of whether there is penetration, we will begin to address the orgasm gap.

Sexual Assault

Any sexual act that occurs without consent. This includes any unwanted touch.

Sexual Harassment

Any unwanted sexual language or nonverbal communication. It includes, but is not limited to, the threat of sexual assault, touching, leering, and catcalling.

Transmen

Men whose gender identity does not align with the sex they were assigned at birth. Gender affirming surgeries are not necessary to claim this identity.

> There are those who question transidentity if persons have not undergone gender affirming surgeries. However, trans identity is NOT dependent on body modifications.

Transwomen

Women whose gender identity does not align with the sex they were assigned at birth. Gender affirming surgeries are not necessary to claim this identity.

Virginity

This is a social construct often used to decide a person's worth or lack thereof. The idea of "losing your virginity" reinforces a sense of worth associated with a lack of sexual engagement. In many cultures, the maintenance of virginity is considered sacred and can be a requirement for young women hoping to marry. Because it is a construct, there is no single way to define it. Some consider those who have engaged in any sexual activity, including mutual masturbation or oral sex, to no longer qualify. For others, disqualification occurs only through penetration of a vagina by a penis. One may see how definitions of virginity can be nonsensical for cis-lesbian and cis-gay couples whose sex practices do not involve penises or vaginas, respectively. I challenge readers who did not experience trauma for their first sexual encounter to redefine the narrative as an experience gained rather than lost.

Vagina versus Vulva

In popular culture, the vulva is called vagina, but they do technically refer to different parts of the body. Vaginas are the internal canal where penetration occurs and through which blood travels for those who menstruate. The blood then exits through the vaginal opening. This is different from the vulva which includes everything you can see if looking at someone who is naked and at least somewhat spread eagled. The vulva includes the labia majora and minora, the clitoral hood and glans, as well as the urethral and vaginal opening.

Womxn

I use this to encapsulate ciswomen and transwomen. Normally I would just say women for both but the specificity of some of the information in this book called for a distinction.

Resources

There are countless resources available in community centers, schools, libraries, the internet, and in those around us. Below are a couple of resources that can be found online, in print, or as in person workshops. For any resource you'd like to use that is not inclusive, make it your own and expand its inclusivity!

Body Image

BodyLove
Different length workshops dedicated to improving relationship with body
Kvibrations.com/events

Diverse Bodies Project
Nude photointerview series challenging beauty norms and diversifying those represented in books and social media
@diversebodiesproject

How I Overcame Colorism and Learned to Love My Dark Skin by Chelsea Odufu: Teen Vogue
One young woman's journey
https://www.teenvogue.com/story/colorism-loving-dark-skin-essay

BDSM

BDSM Friendly professionals: NCS Freedom
https://www.ncsfreedom.org/key-programs/kink-aware-professionals-59776

Quiz for determining your kinky identities

https://bdsmtest.org/select-mode

Fetlife: Social networking space for the kink community
Fetlife.com

I want more kink, but I don't know how to ask a partner for it:
Scarleteen response by Mo Ranyart
*http://www.scarleteen.com/article/advice/i_want_more_kink
_but_i_dont_know_how_to_ask_a_partner_for_it*

Yes/No/Maybe List Sex and Kink by Bex Caputo
Includes a guide, acts, and feelings
*http://www.bextalkssex.com/wp-
content/uploads/2016/10/BexCaputoYesNoMaybe.pdf*

Communication with Others and Self

Be a Blabbermouth! The Whys, Whats and Hows of Talking
About Sex With a Partner: Scarleteen
*http://www.scarleteen.com/article/relationships/be_a_blabb
ermouth_the_whys_whats_and_hows_of_talking_about_sex_wi
th_a_partner*

Love Language Quiz
http://www.5lovelanguages.com/profile/couples/

Ready or Not? The Scarleteen Sex Readiness Checklist by
Heather Corinna
*http://www.scarleteen.com/article/relationships/ready_or_n
ot_the_scarleteen_sex_readiness_checklist*

You Need Help: Here Is A Worksheet To Help You Talk To
Partners About Sex (my favorite list) by A. E. Osworth:
Y/N/M list that goes further by asking about what you want
to be called and includes partner Venn Diagram

https://www.autostraddle.com/you-need-help-here-is-a-worksheet-to-help-you-talk-to-partners-about-sex-237385/

You Feel Like Shit: An Interactive Self-Care Guide
Focuses on communication with self and is meant to be used when one is not feeling well or right
http://philome.la/jace_harr/you-feel-like-shit-an-interactive-self-care-guide/play

Consent

Consent Workshop Resources – KCL Intersectional Feminist Society
https://kclintfemsoc.wordpress.com/consent-workshop-resources/

The Consensual Project
Free workshop manual for teaching consent
http://www.theconsensualproject.com/action/workshop

Teacup Video
Short video that demonstrates respecting consent through a tea analogy
Unedited - *https://www.youtube.com/watch?v=oQbei5JGiT8*
Clean version
https://www.youtube.com/watch?v=fGoWLWS4-kU

Genders and Sexual Orientation

Comprehensive* list of LGBTQ+ vocabulary definitions: It's Pronounced Metrosexual
http://itspronouncedmetrosexual.com/2013/01/a-comprehensive-list-of-lgbtq-term-definitions/
List of genders, sexualities, and their definitions: pbhscloset

http://thepbhscloset.weebly.com/a-list-of-genders--sexualities-and-their-definitions.html

National Center for Transgender Equality:
Website full of informational sheets, know your rights on different topics, and highlights of issues and how they intersect with transidentity
https://transequality.org/

The Safe Zone Project
Curricula for educators and learners on LGBTQ+ topics
https://thesafezoneproject.com/

Pleasure

Fave Trans Products: BexTalksSex
This is for transmasculine folks and is mostly on ways to present as your gender but also includes some talk of masturbatory tools
http://www.bextalkssex.com/fave-trans-products/

Girl Sex 101 by Allison Moon

Lubes 101
http://www.scarleteen.com/article/bodies/lube_101_a_slick_little_primer

The Ultimate Guide to Prostate Pleasure: Erotic Exploration for Men and Their Partners by Charlie Glickman and Aislinn Emirzian

For Yourself: The Fulfillment of Female Sexuality by Dr. Lonnie Barbach

Polyamory

Andie Nordgren's short instructional manifesto for relationship anarchy *http://log.andie.se/*

Sex at Dawn: How We Mate, Why We Stray, and What it Means for Modern Relationships by Christopher Ryan and Cacilda Jethá

The Ethical Slut by Janet W. Hardy and Dossie Easton

Poly-specific Yes/No/Maybe Sheet
http://polynotes.tumblr.com/post/66297551501/poly-yesnomaybe-list

Sexual Assault

National Sexual Violence Resource Center
Free webinars on prevention, restorative justice practice, and more
https://www.nsvrc.org/elearning/college

RAINN (Rape, Abuse & Incest National Network)
Resource page and telephone line for survivors as well as prevention methods.
https://www.rainn.org/

The Complexities of Self-Care After Sexual Assault by Chad Sniffen: National Sexual Violence Resource Center
https://www.nsvrc.org/blogs/complexities-self-care-after-sexual-assault

Sexual Health

Get Birth Control That Works for You: Planned Parenthood
https://www.plannedparenthood.org/planned-parenthood-new-york-city/campaigns/get-birth-control-that-works-for-you?gclid=EAIaIQobChMIufyUnt7O3QIVxJCfCh113QKlEAAYASAAEgKf1vD_BwE

Health and Wellness: Planned Parenthood
https://www.plannedparenthood.org/learn/health-and-wellness

Sexual Health: Center for Disease Control and Prevention (CDC)
Be wary of this source as the government can influence the material
https://www.cdc.gov/sexualhealth/Default.html

The Real Deal On HIV, PrEP, and PEP: Scarleteen
http://www.scarleteen.com/article/sexual_health/the_real_deal_on_hiv_prep_and_pep

More by Scarleteen -
http://www.scarleteen.com/article/sexual-health

Made in the USA
San Bernardino,
CA